CIVIL WAR SEA BATTLES

CIVIL WAR SEA BATTLES

Seafights and Shipwrecks in the War Between the States

Edward Stokes Miller

COMBINED BOOKS
Pennsylvania

Appreciation

I have received invaluable help and advice from two persons, Elizabeth Cadwalader and Frank Duffy, both of whom took time to go over the manuscript and give me invaluable advice. For this I thank them sincerely.

The copyright to Chapter IV and Part 1 of Chapter X is owned by the United States Naval Institute; Chapter II, Part 4 of Chapter X and Chapter XVIII have appeared in *Sea Classics Magazine;* Chapter IX has appeared in *BLUE&GRAY* Magazine. Chapter XIV has appeared and Chapter I will appear in *America's Civil War* and Chapter XVI has appeared in *Civil War Times Illustrated.*

For information, address:
COMBINED BOOKS, INC.
151 E. 10th Avenue
Conshohocken, PA 19428

Library of Congress Cataloging-in-Publication Data
Miller, Edward Stokes, 1917-
Civil War sea battles: seafights and shipwrecks inthe war between states / Edward Stokes Miller.
     p.   cm.
     Includes bibliographical references.
     ISBN 0-938289-52-7
     1. United States—History—Civil War, 1861-1865—Naval operations.   I. Title.
E591.M53   1995
973.7'5—dc20   95-15825   CIP

Combined Books Edition   1   2   3   4   5

First published in the USA in 1995 by Combined Books and distributed in North America by Stackpole Books, Inc., 5067 Ritter Road, Mechanicsburg, PA 17055 and internationally by Greenhill Books, Lionel Leventhal Ltd., 1 Russell Gardens, London NW11 9NN

Printed in the United States of America.

This book is for three people, two of whom will never read it in this world...

First. My beloved wife of over fifty years, Betty, who heroically survived a distaste of history to encourage me and who, being Welsh born, had to overcome a minimum of knowledge and of interest in the American Civil War. She is simply wonderful and I cannot say that enough times.

Second. My grandfather, Lieutenant Commander Edwin Harrison Miller USN (1830-1874). Enlisting in the Navy as a seaman in November 1861, he served in *Constellation* for two years, being promoted to Acting Ensign. Standing fourteenth in the list of officers examined in 1867, he was retained in the service, being promoted in 1870 to the rank of Lieutenant Commander. Victim of a yellow fever epidemic in New Orleans, he died of its complications in 1874 leaving three small children and,

Third. My grandmother, Elizabeth Fisher Miller (1850-1918). Living with her parents in a light house at the Head of the Passes at the mouth of the Mississippi (and thus being a witness to The Fight at the Head of the Passes) she met her future husband in New Orleans where he served at the end of the war. Upon their marriage she moved from Louisiana to the small village of Williamsburg, Massachusetts, light years apart from the urbanity of New Orleans. After her husband's death she returned to New Orleans only to be rejected by her family for having married a Yankee. She moved to Vineland, New Jersey, where she raised her children. Having lived long enough to give me a christening present and dying in the flu epidemic of 1918, of all her contemporaries in this book she is the one I would like most to meet.

Contents

Maps

And some there be, which have no memorial;
Who are perished, as though they had never been;
And become as though they had never been born;
And their children after them.
But these were merciful men,
Whose righteousness hath not been forgotten.
With their seed shall continually remain a good inheritance,
And their children are within the covenant.
Their seed standeth fast,
And their children for their sakes.
Their seed shall remain forever,
And their glory shall not be blotted out.
Their bodies are buried in peace;
But their name liveth for evermore.

Ecclesiasticus 44

Introduction

The Civil War occupies a unique place in America's heart and mind. The turning point in this country's development, it was the logical and inevitable culmination of the principle that a nation which bases its ideals on individual liberty must inevitably extend that liberty to all, regardless of the cost. Since the war was to a large extent a war of volunteers, those who served looked upon their service with pride. One of the more prominent, Oliver Wendell Holmes, told us, "Our hearts were touched with fire" and these sentiments still survive, as witness the continuing interest in all aspects of the war.

The United States Navy grew from 1457 officers and 7,600 men in 1861 to 5,750 officers and 51,500 men in 1865. The vast majority of all ranks was drawn from the professional seamen of the day, either regular navy or the merchant service. They fought the war as well as they knew how and that was very well indeed. They also reported it to their superiors in the language of the time, and they did that very well also. We are fortunate that their language was so simple and clear that it reads today as easily as when it was written. It is from these reports that the following stories were taken. Many of these documents reveal intimate and fascinating details of the events themselves in language striking in its straightforwardness. To anyone accustomed to the technical idiom of the modern military jargon, it is refreshing in its clarity and lack of inhibition. Possibly they had more time to compose their thoughts free from the pressures of modern society, but whatever the reason, these writings of ordinary people are enjoyably readable, from the extravagant prose of Cadwalader Ringgold to the flamboyance of David D. Porter and the sometimes hastily drawn entries in the logbooks.

These stories span that unique period of time when our navy moved from sail-driven wooden frigates to armored steam vessels of all types, from *Governor* to *Monitor*, and from an unprepared service to arguably the strongest naval force in the world. They reflect the monotony and the dangers of naval life on the blockade, (the Union navy's major strategy in subduing the South), and the perils of yellow fever. They also record official reactions, sometimes inequitable, to men in their attempts to serve to the best of their ability.

In an age like ours, when sophistication is the order of the day, it is refreshing to encounter the patriotic insubordination of Quartermaster William Conway, who at least knew his duty when his superiors did not know theirs, and to note his recognition by the navy in later years. And in the case of Acting Master Anthony Chase, it is time the injustice of Admiral David G. Farragut's accusation be corrected. Our country owes that much debt to these men and other forgotten seamen some of whose deeds are recorded in these pages.

—Edward Stokes Miller

CHAPTER I

Quartermaster Conway's Rebellion
Against Rebellion

On 12 January 1861, Commander Ebenezer Farrand USN, executive officer of the Pensacola, Florida, Navy Yard, turned to Quartermaster William Conway, standing by the flagpole, and gave him a direct order to haul down the United States flag flying proudly at its peak. Lowering the flag would mark the Navy Yard's surrender and Farrand's transfer of allegiance from the United States to the State of Florida which had not yet entered the Confederacy. But Quartermaster Conway, whose thirty-eight year naval career matched Farrand's in length of service if not in rank attained, turned to his superior officer and replied, "I will not do it, sir, that is the flag of my country under which I have served many years. I love it and will not dishonor it by hauling it down now." And he did not. Farrand answered this act of defiance by arresting Conway and confining him in chains; Conway's refusal was an act of mutiny. The flag came down and the Pensacola Navy Yard became a Confederate post, but Conway's determination to perform his duty to the United States, despite the consequences, gave early notice of how the North would react to secession and it was an act of bravery which has kept William Conway's name alive to this day.

*   *   *

In the last days of the administration of President James Buchanan, the situation began to look ominous for the Pensacola Navy Yard. The Navy Yard, located on the northern shore of Pensacola's harbor, was the Navy's principal supply and naval base in the Gulf of Mexico. Three Army forts along the harbor's entrance channel— Pickens, Barrancas and McRea—gave the Yard some protection from seaside attacks, as did the two armed ships at the Yard's disposal—the storeship *Supply* and the steamship *Wyandotte*. The Yard's landward defenses consisted only of a ten-foot wall and some artillery pieces: twenty-two 18 pounder cannon, eight 32 pounders, two 8 inch guns, and a saluting battery of one functioning gun. This firepower should have been enough to protect the Yard and its approaches, except that the only gun mounted was the saluting battery, and it was in such poor condition that one of its carriages fell apart while firing a salute. However, the Yard did have sufficient ammunition (probably intended to supply visiting warships) and it could have had the guns operating and the Yard in condition to resist attack were it not for its commander's indecision.

Captain James Armstrong USN, who had been on active duty since the year in which Abraham Lincoln was born, had assumed command of the Yard on 30 October 1860. His two principal subordinates were his executive officer, Ebenezer Farrand, and Lieutenant Francis B. Renshaw, Farrand's brother-in-law. Both these officers openly favored the Confederacy and although many of their like-minded contemporaries performed their duties loyally down to the moment they resigned their commissions, Farrand and Renshaw did everything in their power to prevent placing the Yard in a state of defense and the vacillating Armstrong was unable to handle them. The Yard's other personnel included forty-one marines (Captain of Marines Josiah Watson, eight noncommissioned officers and thirty-two privates), a boatswain, a storekeeper, a master machinist, various other technicians, and eighty "men in ordinary," (probably non-rated sailors).

Trouble broke out on 9 January. Armstrong received an order that day from the Secretary of the Navy directing him to "protect the public property" and to cooperate with the local army commander, First Lieutenant Adam Slemmer, then at Fort Barrancas. Slemmer, his adjutant, and Armstrong all agreed that Fort Pickens, the largest and most formidable of the three Army posts, was the only one which was defensible. The other forts were abandoned; Armstrong sent men to help move troops, arms and ammunition to Pickens and to help garrison the fort. However, they were unable to transport all the powder, which included twenty-two thousand pounds at the third fort, McCrea. Lieutenant Henry Erben of *Supply* destroyed the powder which could not be moved and then offered to destroy the powder and stores in the Navy Yard as well.

Erben's action enraged Farrand. He confronted the lieutenant in front of Armstrong, accusing Erben of being drunk and demanding his arrest. Reading from Armstrong's instructions, Farrand shouted at Erben, "Do you call this protecting public property by destroying it?" yelling loudly enough to prompt a reprimand from Armstrong. At the same time Renshaw insisted that Armstrong send the *Supply* to Vera Cruz, Mexico, and the *Wyandotte* to Cuba; Armstrong refused both their demands, probably because it would have scattered the available fighting ships.

At this, Farrand lost any remnants of self-control. He threw a chair at Erben and stormed out of the room. An irate Erben followed him and, once outside, Farrand accosted him, "Damn you, I'll teach you how to treat your superior officers."

"Damn *you*, I'll have you hanged as a traitor, as you are," Erben replied. The two men began to fight; others who opposed Farrand joined in and both Farrand and Renshaw abandoned the fight, defeated.

By 11 January it was clear to the men at the Yard that trouble was coming to a head. Farrand nonetheless declined to place the "ordinary" men under arms, on the grounds that "from their dissolute character they would be more dangerous to those inside the yard than the persons without," strange logic considering that

Quartermaster William Conway, as sketched by Alfred Waud.

the prime danger to the Yard was the team of Farrand and Renshaw. The following day, close to noon, three to four hundred lightly armed volunteers from Florida and Alabama appeared outside the yard's front gate. Two "commissioners" entered the Yard, were met by Farrand and demanded the Yard be surrendered to them. Farrand's response was to direct the invaders to the powder magazine, thus depriving the Yard of the means of resistance. He could not have disarmed the Yard any more effectively had he caused all its arms and ammunition to vanish into thin air. He then conducted the "commissioners" to Armstrong. They confronted him with the same demand—that he surrender the Yard to the State of Florida.

Armstrong had already failed to make adequate preparations for the Yard's defense; now he declined to offer any resistance. He handed the Southerners the keys to the magazine and ordered his marines to stack their arms, the last order of his naval career. Although "all of the men seemed very reluctant to obey—they were very much affected, some of them to tears and said they would not obey; they would not suffer the humiliation; they would sooner be shot."[1]— Armstrong's final order was obeyed.

The Pensacola Naval Yard had fallen without a shot fired and without resistance from any of its officers. However, one man refused to give up so readily. Quartermaster William Conway, from Camden, Maine, had served in the Navy for many years. As quartermaster, he was responsible for the colors—the United States ensign flying over the Yard. Following Armstrong's surrender, in the midst of the troops now occupying the Yard, Conway was ordered by Farrand to strike the flag, which order he refused.

He took his life in his hands when he refused to haul down the flag. As Erben put it, "the order was given by an officer with a United States commission in his pocket. He was surrounded by a crazed crowd, made so by the surrender of the yard, a most important depot. Conway was threatened to be cut down [on the spot] but he still refused to haul down the flag he had served under for so many years."[2] The immediate response to Conway's defiant act was his arrest. He was clapped into chains and Farrand himself lowered the Stars and Stripes. As the flag was coming down, Marine Captain Watson said to Renshaw, "I had hoped I would never live to see the day when that would happen."

Renshaw replied, "I am not hauling it down to an enemy; I am hauling it down to our own people."

The Yard was then turned over to the Florida State representatives.

The advantages which the Confederacy gained by taking the Pensacola Navy Yard were the capture of its ordnance materiel and its unavailability to the Union forces. As an offensive base, the yard was useless without control of the army forts. On 12 April—the day Fort Sumter was fired on—*Brooklyn* and *Sabine* arrived off Fort Pickens to blockade the harbor; this blockade continued until

USS Sabine, *one of the ships that blockaded Pensacola after its capture by the Confederates. Many of her crew later served on the* Monitor.

the recapture of Pensacola on 10 May 1862. The Yard remained in Confederate hands but a year and three months.

The Yard may not have been a great gain to the Confederacy, but its loss had serious consequences for the Union officers responsible. Farrand and Renshaw, whose sympathies were already with the South, resigned from the navy almost immediately after the Yard fell, and both served in the Confederate navy during the war. Conway and those officers loyal to the Union were released soon thereafter and returned North on unilaterally imposed "paroles." A "parole" by a captive prisoner is an agreement not to bear arms against the capturing power until duly exchanged as a prisoner of war, and is thus a contract between the parties. No Union officer or enlisted man at Pensacola agreed to any such terms and the so-called "paroles" were invalid as such.

Within a month, Captain Armstrong faced a court martial. One could sympathize with Armstrong, then sixty-seven years old, laboring under ambiguous and uninspiring directions from Buchanan's administration in Washington. Nonetheless, the court convicted him of dereliction of duty and sentenced him to a public reprimand and suspension for five years, the first two and a half without pay. He never served again.

Of all the participants, Quartermaster Conway fared the best. The same court martial that condemned Armstrong called attention to Conway's conduct in a separate communication to the new Secretary of the Navy, Gideon Welles. Welles issued a general order on April 24, 1861, which pointed out that Conway had "indignantly refused to obey" Farrand's order and then went on:

> The love and reverence thus impulsively exhibited for his country's flag in the hour of its perils is not the less worthy of being called noble and chivalric because displayed by one in an humble station. It is the more deserving of commemoration, for subordinates in the service are not usually expected to set examples of patriotism and fidelity in their trusts, but to follow them.[3]

Welles directed that this order be read aloud "as early as practicable after its receipt by the commanders of all naval stations and all vessels in commission, in the presence of all the officers and men under their command." In addition, 148 Californians subscribed for a medal "of California gold" and sent it to Washington to be presented to Conway as a mark of their appreciation. By then, Conway was serving as quartermaster aboard USS *Mississippi*, part of the Gulf Squadron commanded by Flag Officer William W. McKean. Welles directed McKean to present the medal to Conway "on the quarterdeck of the vessel to which he belongs, and in the presence of the officers and crew thereof." When it was reported that Conway had tears in his eyes during the presentation, he declared that, if so, it was not because he was affected sentimentally but because he was either mad or had a cold.

During his naval career Conway remained true to form. On board *Mississippi* with him was Lieutenant—later Admiral—George Dewey. Dewey relates:

> When I had become Executive Officer of the *Mississippi* and she...had passed the forts below New Orleans in April, 1862, I looked at the other vessels and saw that [they] were firing broadsides with Old Glory at each masthead... [I]t had not occurred to me to have the flags hoisted. Conway was standing near me and as he had charge of the flags I said, "Get out our flags quickly, Conway." He replied, "They're up there, sir." Without waiting for instructions he had hoisted them up in balls waiting to be broken out at a moment's notice, thus showing more forethought in that respect than either the Captain or myself.*

Conway continued to serve in the navy throughout the war. He died, still on active duty, on 30 November 1865, in the Brooklyn Naval Hospital; he was sixty years old. His funeral procession was accompained by four commodores. For many men, recognition comes too late; it is nice to know that Conway received praise for his actions in time for him to enjoy it.

Although, sadly, his grave was not marked and cannot be found today, his memory at least has been kept alive. In 1906 his home town of Camden, Maine, unveiled a memorial plaque in recognition of his loyalty. This plaque, which is still there, reads as follows:

---

* Conway seems to have had his share of dry Yankee humor, for Dewey went on to relate: On a certain 22nd of February, after the abolition of the grog ration I saw Conway, who had been in the habit of taking his grog twice a day for many years. Touching his cap he said to me, "It's a mighty dry birthday for poor old George Washington, Mr. Dewey."

William Conway
Quartermaster, U.S. Navy
a native of Camden
On duty at the Pensacola Navy Yard Jan. 12, 1861
Was ordered to haul down the American flag
in token of surrender
He indignantly refused
Honoring his sturdy loyalty
The town of Camden erects this boulder
to his memory and
The Maine Commandery of the Military Order
Of the Loyal Legion of the United States
Adds this tablet
1906

Present for the ceremony was the entire North Atlantic Fleet complement of twelve battleships under the command of Rear Admiral Robley D. Evans (himself a severely wounded veteran of the Civil War), who ordered a national salute of twenty-one guns to be fired in Conway's honor.

This was not all. In November, 1939, by order of President Franklin D. Roosevelt, Destroyer No. 70, formerly USS *Craven*, was renamed *Conway* in his honor. After being commissioned on 9 August she was turned over to the British Navy on 23 October 1940 as a part of the U. S. Lend-Lease program, and served therein as HMS *Lewes*. Conway's name, however, continued in the United States Navy when, on 9 October 1942, Destroyer No. 507 was commissioned as USS *Conway* and served during and many years after the Second World War. Happily, in Camden, Maine, his old homestead is still in service as the headquarters of the Camden-Rockport Historical Society.

CHAPTER II

The Fight at the Head of the Passes

At the start of the Civil War the United States Navy found itself in a serious crisis. Decimated by large numbers of its best officers resigning to "go South" to join the new Confederacy, it soon discovered that the ships it possessed were not the type of vessels required to enforce the blockade which President Lincoln sought to impose upon the South (against the advice of his Secretary of the Navy Gideon Welles). It was also inevitable that the service would suffer greatly from growing pains, until the ships were found and officers and men trained to man them. The first year of the war was an unhappy one for the hard pressed Navy and its Secretary.

*   *   *

When the United States Navy entered the Civil War, it had been forty-six years since its last major conflict, against the British Navy in the War of 1812. True, it had engaged in skirmishes around the world from the shores of Tripoli to the Far East, and the country had fought a war with Mexico, but Mexico had no navy. Forty-six years without fighting had produced an officer corps of skilled mariners which was deficient in combat experience. Witness the case of Captain John Pope of USS *Richmond* and Commander Robert Handy of USS *Vincennes*.

Pope entered the navy as a midshipman in 1816 and spent ten years in that subordinate rank, becoming a lieutenant in 1826. He spent seventeen years in that rank and twelve years as a commander before finally making captain in July 1855. Handy began as a midshipman in 1826, spent eleven years in that rank and eighteen years as a lieutenant, before being promoted to commander in 1855. Although neither career was calculated to prepare for or develop leadership, in the summer of 1861 Pope was in command of *Richmond*, and Handy in command of *Vincennes* on blockading duty at the mouth of the Mississippi River in the Gulf of Mexico.

Vincennes, a sailing sloop of war, had been laid down in 1825, eleven months before Handy had become a midshipman. Armed with four 8 inch and fourteen 32 pounder guns, with a draft of fifteen feet, with her deep water design, and with her lack of mechanical propulsion, she was completely unfit for duty amid the shoals and sand bars of the Gulf Coast. That she was so employed was proof positive of the poverty of the United States Navy.

Even if she had possessed the right qualifications, the duty assigned her and her consorts would have tested her to the limit; it involved the blockade of New Orleans, Louisiana, and the entrances to the Mississippi River, a task which eventually consumed the services of an entire fleet. The geography of the region presented no small obstacle to a blockading force. The Mississippi River system, draining the central portion of the continental United States, passes through the channels and major port of New Orleans about one hundred miles before it enters the Gulf of Mexico. The topography may have changed somewhat since that war, but the geography remains much the same. The current still runs past the city at between two and one-half and four miles per hour just as it did during the Civil War.

On the east bank of the river some sixty five miles below New Orleans, the Spaniards had long ago built stone Fort St. Philip. Impelled by the War of 1812, the Americans had then built, and later improved, a brick and masonry structure, Fort Jackson, on the west bank opposite Fort St. Philip. With only a mile and a half of river between them, it was believed that these emplacements made entry of a hostile force into New Orleans impossible.

For some twenty miles below the forts, the river runs in a straight line south to where it divides into three channels, resembling the claw of a giant bird and known in Southern terminology as "passes." These three passes were, and are, the principal access to New Orleans and the central portion of the continent. They were strategically vital to both the Union and the Confederacy.

At the conjunction of the three channels stood a lighthouse and a small settlement and pilot station known as the Head of the Passes. The broad expanse of the river and the excellent anchorage it afforded made this site a crucial one, commanding the entrance to the river and the vast continent beyond. From this central point a mariner outward bound has his choice of which pass he may use to take his departure; conversely, an inbound vessel, regardless of which pass she has used, must necessarily clear the Head of the Passes before she continues upstream.

The westerly, or South West Pass, had formerly been the deepest and most popular of the passes but had become less so after 1852, when the sand bar at the entrance found at the mouth of all such passes silted up to the point where it was a hazard to navigation. At the onset of the war, the depth of water over that bar was a little over 13 feet, becoming a great obstacle to the Federal Navy whose most effective vessels were of such deep draft that they could not enter the Mississippi River. Those deep sea vessels that did, Flag Officer David G. Farragut's flagship *Hartford* for example, were able to do so only by off loading much of their equipment and being dragged through the mud across the bar into deep water.

The center or South Pass was the shallowest and least used of the three, although it did permit usage by small vessels and so required constant guarding against escaping raiders. Running in a general southeasterly direction from the junction was the second most important channel, known as Pass à l'Outre, which complicated the work of the blockaders by dividing itself into two channels, so that the unfortunate Yankees were required to patrol not three, but four, exits.

All this was, of course, well known to Secretary of the Navy

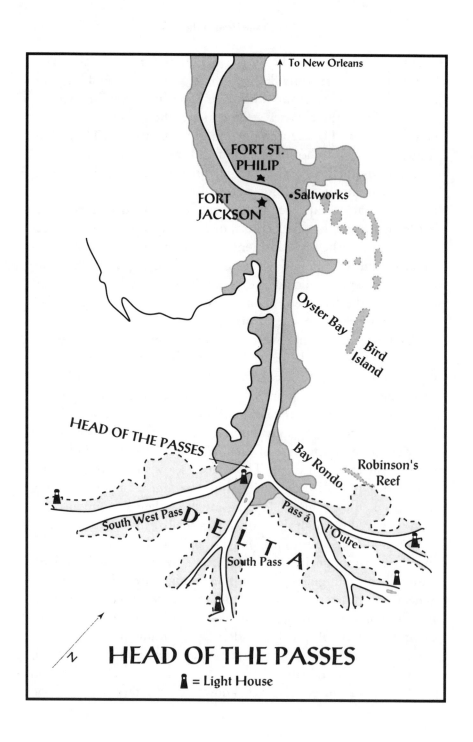

To New Orleans

FORT ST. PHILIP

•Saltworks

FORT JACKSON

Oyster Bay

Bird Island

HEAD OF THE PASSES

Bay Rondo

Robinson's Reef

South West Pass

D E L T A

Pass à l'Outre

South Pass

N

HEAD OF THE PASSES

= Light House

Gideon Welles, Lincoln's strong-willed Secretary of the Navy. His highly personal direction of naval affairs was an important factor in the Union war effort.

Gideon Welles. At the onset of the war, Welles had appointed a committee of experienced officers headed by Captain Samuel F. Du Pont and charged it with the duty of preparing a detailed analysis of the coastline of the Confederacy and recommendation of measures for effectively blockading it.[1] That body recommended the capture and complete fortification of the Head of the Passes, a necessary and proper step but an impossible one for the harassed secretary at the outset of the war, since it required more force than he had available at that time.

Welles did the best he could with what he had; he sent a few blockaders to guard the entrances to the passes and created at least a paper blockade. It worked, but not very effectively; although he had at least one vessel at the entrance to each pass, they were unable to completely stop the leaks. At the end of June 1861, with all passes supposedly blocked, Raphael Semmes took CSS *Sumter* down to Pass à l'Outre, somehow avoiding detection by USS *Brooklyn,* and when that hapless Federal took off in chase of a strange sail, got *Sumter* safely away, commencing a commerce raiding career which inscribed Semmes' name in naval history forever.

By the end of summer, Welles had assembled what he hoped was a force of sufficient strength to commence implementing the committee's recommendations. He sent to the mouth of the Mississippi a force of four vessels, of which Pope was the senior officer (in modern terms, in tactical command). This force consisted of the following vessels:

Richmond, a 225 foot screw sloop, mounting fourteen 9 inch smooth bore guns, under the command of Pope.

Water Witch, a 150 foot side wheel sloop, mounting one 32 pounder, under the command of Lieutenant Francis Winslow.

Preble, a 117 foot sailing sloop, mounting two 8 inch and seven 32 pounders, under the command of Commander Henry French.

Vincennes, the other sailing vessel, under Handy.

Of the four, only *Richmond* could pass muster as a viable warship, and she labored under the handicap of being what admiralty lawyers call "constrained by her draft" of seventeen and a half feet, guaranteed to cause problems crossing a thirteen foot bar. *Water Witch* had achieved some distinction when she had spent some three years surveying the rivers of South America, scarcely a test of combat effectiveness. Both *Preble* and *Vincennes* were as outdated as the dinosaurs.

On 19 September *Water Witch* entered Pass à l'Outre and ascended to the Head of the Passes to learn whether it was feasible to construct an artillery battery there. Before arriving at her destination she discovered an armed schooner lying at anchor and observed the smoke of a steamer ascending the South West Pass, an indication that possession of the area would not be undisputed.[2]

Confederate Secretary of the Navy Stephen Mallory. He did a remarkable job assembling an improvised Confederate navy.

The Confederate command was neither inattentive nor lazy. Secretary of the Navy Stephen R. Mallory had placed Captain George S. Hollins CSN in command to organize the defense of the river and the Head of the Passes. By the time the Federals had completed their preparations to occupy that strategic spot, Hollins was ready for them. The force he was able to put together was indeed formidable for the time and place. He assembled:

CSS *Calhoun*, a 175 foot side wheel steamer, mounting one 30 pounder rifle and two 32 pounder Dahlgren guns, previously employed as a privateer.

Ivy, another side wheel steamer, 191 feet in length and mounting one 8 inch smooth bore and one 32 pounder rifle and two 24 pounders.

Jackson, another side wheeler, mounting two 32 pounders.

McCrae, a steam gunboat, mounting one 9 inch and six 32 pounder smooth bores and possessing the dubious distinction of having been a gunboat in the Mexican navy which had been seized as a pirate by USS *Saratoga* in 1860 and caught at New Orleans by the outbreak of the war.

In addition, Hollins possessed the side wheel steamer *Tuscarora* with one 32 pounder and the former United States Revenue Cutter *Robert McClelland*, a sailing schooner.

This assortment composed almost entirely of steam vessels was formidable enough in its own right to oppose Pope's meager squadron of two steam and two sailing vessels. However, Hollins possessed still another asset, which, by itself, should have been able to take on the entire Federal force: the steam ram *Manassas*, the true ancestor of American armored warships. Commissioned and operational a full nine months earlier than her famous step-sister CSS *Virginia*, ex-USS *Merrimack*, she was 143 feet in length and had been converted from the towboat *Enoch Train*. Covered with an inch and half of iron, she was a formidable opponent, made even more so by the aura of mystery in which the incomplete intelligence of the day surrounded her. In the drawings of her which have survived, she looks curiously modern, with her freeboard, or height above the water, a mere two feet, six inches, a curved turtle shaped deck and sharp bow, quaintly resembling a modern submarine. Armed with but one 64 pounder gun, she was designed primarily to be used as a ram in the fashion of the Greek and Roman galleys of bygone times.

After struggling for several days to go up stream by way of Pass à l'Outre, on September 23 Pope decided to attempt the Southwest Pass and consumed a week getting his little force over the bar. *Richmond* seems to have got across without too much difficulty; *Vincennes* had more trouble. On September 29 *Water Witch* tried to tow her over the bar and failed; two days later *Vincennes* tried again, grounded on a wreck for another two days, and finally got over on October 3, when she was towed to the Head of the Passes where the little flotilla assembled to await developments.

Pope seems to have paid little attention to the defense of his squadron beyond some rather feeble efforts to place artillery on shore. His squadron merely anchored and stood by; the delay was just long enough for Hollins to assemble his forces and come down to greet them.

The first attack came on the afternoon of 9 October. *Vincennes'* log records:

> [F]rom 4 to 6. A steamer came down the river and opened fire upon us which was returned by the different ships. We fired 3 shot and 3 shells, all of which fell short. The steamer's shot passed clear over us. The Commander signalled to us to hold our fire until nearer. He afterwards signalled "cease firing."

Apparently Pope was impressed by the fact that shot from the Confederate vessel (*Ivy* with her 8 inch gun and one 32 pounder rifle) had passed over and beyond his ships. He apparently failed to realize that if *Ivy's* shot could pass beyond his ships, *Ivy* herself simply had to be within range of his own heavier guns.

The result of this skirmish was to put the wind up Pope, who forthwith fired off a letter to Flag Officer William W. McKean, commanding the Gulf Blockading Squadron. The degree of his panic may be judged by his language:

> We are liable to be driven from here at any moment, and, situated as we are, our position is untenable. I may be captured at any moment by a pitiful little steamer mounting only one gun. It would be the height of folly to send coal or provisions, as they could not be taken on board under the fire of the enemy.[3]

This report from the commander of a ship mounting no less than fourteen 9 inch guns, all of them heavier than the 8 inch gun carried by *Ivy*, and reinforced by the rest of the ships present, impelled McKean to promptly call for reinforcements, but before anything could be done about it, the Confederates struck again.

On 12 October 1861, the midnight watch aboard *Richmond* was engaged in coaling ship. (That Pope caused this monotonous and back-breaking task to be undertaken during the dark hours of the night, thus ruining his crew's rest, gives some indication of his state of mind.) The attention of the weary watch may have been numbed by this activity; at any rate at 3:45 a.m. a vessel was discovered close aboard. It was *Manassas,* and her sighting was the beginning of an action which was to become the third fleet action ever to be fought by the United States Navy, the first fought under steam and with armor and, incidently, the first to be lost!*

Manassas slammed into the unfortunate *Richmond,* striking her on the port side abreast her foremast, driving a hole in her side and ripping asunder the lines which held her fast to the coal schooner. Passing downstream with the current, the ram again struck *Richmond,* but less successfully. The net result was that three planks were stove in about two feet below the water line, making a hole about five inches in circumference. Annoying as this no doubt was, it presented little danger to *Richmond,* whose experienced crew got to action stations soon enough to discharge her entire port battery into *Manassas.* The pivotal consequence, however, was the effect it had on Pope, confronted not only with *Manassas,* but now with three burning rafts which Hollins was drifting down on them. Without taking time for a proper evaluation of the situation, he caused a red light to be shown at the masthead as a signal of danger and ordered the squadron to slip their cables and run.

Aboard *Water Witch,* whose commander and crew seem to have kept their heads, there appears little indication of the tension which must have existed. Her log records succinctly:

At 3.50 a.m. saw a Rebel steamer run into the U.S. ship *Rich-*

---

* Not counting skirmishes in the Mediterranean in 1815 and 1816 where the enemy was simply outclassed. The others were the battles of Lake Erie and Lake Champlain in the War of 1812.

mond but caused no damage...[T]he whole fleet beat to quarters & fired into the iron plated steamer. She succeeded in getting away. At 4 a.m. she [*Richmond*] sent up a rocket. We then saw several lights in the air some spread into a large fire supposed to be hulks chained together, filled with combustibles to fire the U.S. vessels. The fleet slip'd cables & proceeded to the SW Pass...At 4.10 slipped our cable & stood across the river & back till 5:30 when we started down the SW Pass in search of the fleet pursued by 4 steam gun boats. One large bark rigged do [ditto].

Aboard *Vincennes* things did not proceed as calmly. The quartermaster who drew up the log was sufficiently impressed with the occasion to give the day's events a title; at the top of the entry for 12 October appear the words "The fight at the Head of the Passes." The rest of the page tells the story:

At 4 the *Richmond* stood towards us, and hailed us to get under way, and stood down the river. A fire ship was discovered, coming directly down upon us. Veered to 30 fathoms shackle on the port chain and then slipped our cable... We fired a broadside with our port battery into the "fire raft." Our head being fairly pointed down the stream we made sail to topsails and jib and cut the hawser, set topgallant sails and foresail. The "fire raft" began to blaze fiercely and we observed that it was made of three flat boats or hulks chained together, the interval between each being about 200 feet. It lit the way for us, and by it we directed our ship fairly into the SW Pass.

By the skillful use of his available force, Hollins had mastered the Union vessels and had regained control of the entrances to the Mississippi. There can be no evasion of the unpleasant truth: the Confederates had inflicted a significant defeat upon the luckless Federals, not only defeating but routing them. But Hollins was not yet finished. Before he concluded, he was to inflict not only defeat but ridicule on his adversaries.

The kindest way to put it is to say the Union vessels proceeded down the South West Pass to the bar followed by the Confederates;

the plain unvarnished truth is that they were chased downstream and considered themselves lucky to get away. Hollins, however, did not chase too vigorously, for he knew what he was up against; he had spent forty-seven years in the Old Navy, the last six as a captain before leaving the service to "go South." Since the officers of the old service had been such a closely knit "band of brothers," it is probable that Hollins knew the minds of his adversaries well. So, while he pursued the Federals from a discreet distance, never giving the heavy artillery of *Richmond* and *Vincennes* a chance to pound him, pound *them* he did.

Daybreak found the fleeing Federals at the bar, confronted not only with their pursuers but the navigational difficulties of the bar itself. *Preble* and *Water Witch* got across safely; *Richmond* and *Vincennes* were not so lucky. Both of them grounded, immovable targets for Hollins and his flotilla. This proved too much for Handy's nerves, impaired his judgment and robbed him of his common sense.

Forgetting that, although aground and immobile, both *Richmond* and *Vincennes* retained all their fighting capacity, he persuaded himself that he was in greater danger than he actually was, that the cause was irretrievably lost, and that his vessel was unsalvageable. This precipitated a tragi-comic incident which eventually cost him his command and made him the laughing stock of the service.

He started out well enough; finding that since his vessel's head was pointed downstream, thus making it impossible to bring his broadside guns to bear, he had two of his 8 inch shell guns moved to the stern ports from whence they could reach the enemy and began efforts to free his grounded ship from the mud. But when Hollins' flotilla opened fire on him he lost his judgment and sent this doleful message to Pope:

> SIR: We are aground. We have only two guns that will bear in the direction of the enemy. Shall I remain on board after the moon goes down, with my crippled ship and worn-out men? Will you

send me word what countersign my boats shall use if we pass your ship? While we have moonlight, would it not be better to leave the ship? Shall I burn her when I leave her?[4]

This plaintive message acted like a tonic upon Pope, who was beginning to regain his composure. He straightaway fired back a reply to Handy:

> You say your ship is aground. It will be your duty to defend your ship up to the last moment, and not to fire her, except it be to prevent her from falling into the hands of the enemy.
> I do not think the enemy will be down tonight, but in case they do, fight them to the last. You have boats enough to save all your men. I do not approve of your leaving your ship until every effort to defend her from falling into their hands is made.

In addition to the written message, Pope ordered a message to be sent by means of coded flag signals. It is not clear what that message was; *Richmond*'s log is lost and reports from *Vincennes* are confusing. Handy, by now completely unnerved, read the flags as Signal No. 1, the command to abandon ship, a signal vigorously denied by Pope and never really confirmed by anybody else aboard *Vincennes*. Whether or not Handy was correct, he gave the order to abandon ship. The log:

> Hoisted out the 1st and 2d cutters and launch and lowered the stern and quarter boats. Still on the bar with topsails, topgallant sails and jib set...This ship being between the fire of the *Richmond* and the Rebel steamers, at about 11:20 abandoned ship. (in obedience to signal from the *Richmond**) and with the remainder of our crew went to the *Richmond*. Put slow match to the magazine when the boats left the ship. The Rebel steamers getting nearer to us and keeping up a heavy fire upon us from the moment of abandonment. Kept up a constant fire from our stern guns. The last gun fired was disabled (the rear axle breaking off without breeching.)

The asterisk (*) commemorates an episode unique in the history of the Navy. It was inserted in the log by the officer of the deck,

Acting Lieutenant Edgar Brodhead, who then wrote in the log in his own handwriting:

> Note—I did not see the *Richmond* make signal No. 1. Was informed by Capt. Handy that she did so. E. Brodhead.*

It is worthwhile pondering the implications of this statement. By inserting this defiant statement in the log, the official record of the ship, Brodhead in effect called his superior a liar on the record. Interestingly enough, when the compilers of the *Official Records* prepared the reports of this event,[5] they felt compelled to print out extracts from *Vincennes'* log; Brodhead's insert does *not* appear.

Notwithstanding any argument which might have taken place on *Vincennes*, and the fact that he had sent a boat to *Preble* and been informed by her that the signal was not to abandon ship but merely to get under way, Handy then proceeded to abandon ship. After ordering a slow match laid to the powder magazine, he and his crew departed, going either to *Water Witch* or to *Richmond*. He, himself, went aboard the flagship.

Handy's entry caused a stir. For some unfathomable reason Handy had procured the large American flag that was *Vincennes'* ensign and draped it about his body as if it were a Roman toga. His appearance through the entrance port in the manner of Imperial Caesar was the final straw for Pope, and the end of Handy's usefulness as a naval officer.

When *Vincennes* failed to explode, Pope told Handy to get himself and his crew back aboard their vessel and do their duty. On returning to the ship it was discovered that the slow match had mysteriously gone out, leaving a strong suspicion that some cooler head than Handy's had put it out. Handy then put the finishing touches on his career. He caused all fourteen of his 32 pounders to be thrown overboard!

---

* Actually the log contains a second statement that *Richmond* made signal No. 1 and Brodhead put an asterisk by that statement as well.

By this time Hollins, who knew better than to get in a slugging match with Pope's heavier cannon, decided it was time to go home. This he did to the plaudits of his country. He had earned them, for he had done a great deal for the Confederacy and had staved off the inevitable surrender of New Orleans for a considerable time to come. He has never really been given credit for his accomplishments: the first use of armor; victory in the Confederacy's first fleet action, and the first real victory over the United States Navy since HMS *Shannon* took USS *Chesapeake* in the War of 1812.

Pope lost little time in getting rid of Handy. Two days later, after all his vessels had cleared the bar safely, he wrote a letter to McKean quaintly marked "Private in part." In it he said:

> I am sorry to say it but the truth must be told, and that is, Handy is not fit to command a ship; particulars I have not the time to enter into. He is a laughingstock of all and everyone. I do not know what you can do in the case.

McKean knew exactly what to do. On October 28 Lieutenant Samuel Marcy joined *Vincennes* and forthwith relieved Handy, who sailed for the North two days later. However, for some unstated reason, despite the relief on the 28th, Marcy did not publish his orders to the crew until November 3, by which time Handy was several hundred miles away.

Marcy's tour as commander of *Vincennes* was brief, however. When he fell ill some three months later, he was relieved of command by the same Lieutenant Brodhead who had placed his defiant denial in the log. Most flag officers are nobody's fool and McKean must have known what the true facts were.

In the long run Hollins' victory, complete as it was, proved sterile. The next summer Farragut came up to the Head of the Passes, ran past the forts, destroying the dauntless *Manassas* in the process, and took New Orleans itself, wrenching it from the Confederacy forever.

* * *

The battle is reported in ORN I, 16, pp. 703 to 730a which includes copies of the reports in the Southern press. Only the deck logs of *Vincennes* and *Water Witch* survive in the National Archives. Brodhead's defiant entry in *Vincennes'* log stands out like a sore thumb.

CHAPTER III

The Rescue from the *Governor*

The United States Navy entered the Civil War at a time when the service was in a period of transition from sail to steam and from wood to iron. Of the ninety vessels in the naval register, fifty were wooden sailing vessels, only sixteen of which were in commission. Another sixteen were unserviceable and the remainder were either laid up "in ordinary" or used as receiving ships. Used primarily to show the flag in foreign waters, none saw combat during the war; by 1864 they were discarded except as storeships or receiving ships. The old frigate *Constellation*, for example, returning that year from a two year cruise in the Mediterranean reported to Rear Admiral David G. Farragut for duty off Mobile Bay, Alabama. Farragut's immediate decision was to transfer part of her crew to his own ships and send her forthwith to Norfolk, Virginia, where she was decommissioned and became a barracks ship. The other side of the coin, however, is that, obsolete or not, the ships were used and used successfully until more modern steam replacements became available. And at times they still proved equal to their younger sisters, witness the case of USS *Sabine*.

Sabine and her sister, *Santee*, were descendants of the famous 44 gun cruisers of the early 1800s, of which the great frigate *Constitution* was the prototype. These early frigates had been some of the most powerful warships in the world; *Sabine* was enlarged and made even more powerful. Whereas *Constitution* had been given the 175 foot length and the inner strength of a battleship of that period, *Sabine* was built to a length of 202 feet and strengthened accordingly. Laid down in 1823 although, surprisingly, not launched until 1855, she was the last and most powerful vessel of the American sailing navy.

*   *   *

On the afternoon of Friday, 1 November 1861, the Union steamer *Governor* was laboring heavily in a violent storm somewhere off the South Carolina coast. Chartered by the navy for use as a troop transport, the privately owned ship had embarked a battalion of Marines and sailed from Hampton Roads, Virginia, on 29 October in company with a fleet of fifty vessels bent on the capture of Port Royal, South Carolina. The expedition was designed to obtain a naval base where blockading vessels could seek shelter and supplies and from which Union forces could advance into Confederate territory.

Overcoming the navy's unreadiness for war a scant six months earlier, its rudimentary staff, and its undeveloped planning procedures, Flag Officer Samuel F. Du Pont and his officers had assembled a massive force. Even the best planners, however, could not control one element—the weather. Along the coast of the Carolinas and Virginia in October and November, warm, balmy days can give way to near hurricanes. In the last days of October 1861, one of these unexpected tempests played havoc with Du Pont's fleet.

The expedition had departed in uncertain weather and by the time the fleet reached Cape Hatteras the wind was blowing hard, driving several vessels so far in to the beach as the breakers, where two actually struck bottom before managing to escape. On Friday, November 1, the gale force winds reached near hurricane velocity,

Veteran crewmen of the USS Mendota *early in the war. The British and American navies had an ethnic mix unknown in land forces of the time.*

what would today be called a whole gale. *Governor* was doomed; her captain, C.L. Litchfield, unnerved.

About 11 a. m. part of the vessel's bracing collapsed, terrifying Litchfield so badly that he lost control of his nerves and permitted Acting Master John Weidman, a naval officer on board as a passenger, to take command. Weidman found the ship in deep trouble. *Governor's* sponsors were leaky and unseaworthy, her hull nearly as bad, her pumps in "wretched order" and unable to contain the two feet of water in the hold.[1]

Weidman took immediate and effective action. First, he altered course to bring the wind behind him and ease *Governor's* reaction to the sea, although this meant abandoning the fleet and, temporarily, his mission. He found the crew little, if any, help. "...[T]he least I can say is that they were very, very worthless. The chief engineer and the chief mate conducted themselves as cowards and traitors only know how." He compensated for the crew's deficiencies both by having the pumps repaired and by using the Marines as a bucket brigade. These measures controlled the flooding, but his hope of success soon faded.

That night the winds escalated, shifting to the south and *Governor* floundered. "Several accidents succeeded each other in quick succession, soon after culminating in the fall of the smokestack, the bursting of the steam pipe, and the vessel becoming unmanageable." Without the draft from the smokestack, the fires to the boiler could not be kept up or steam pressure to the engine maintained; the pumps began to fail, and Weidman confided to Major John G. Reynolds, the Marine commander, that he had little hope of coming through safely.

Although the fleet had scattered, the sheer number of ships in the expedition meant that *Governor* would not stay alone for long. During the morning of the 2d, she met the gunboat *Isaac Smith*, which tried in vain to pass a line to her. During these attempts the auxiliary bark *Young Rover* came alongside to report that the frigate *Sabine* was on the way. Yet the wind was so strong and the sea so rough that her arrival did not ensure the *Governor's* rescue.

Both *Sabine* and her commander, Captain Cadwalader Ringgold, were products of the "Old Navy"—the sailing navy. Though a master of seamanship, Ringgold had no experience with steam vessels. His career in the navy spanned forty-seven years but in this war wherein the age of sail and wood gave way to that of steam and iron, he never commanded anything other than this one sailing vessel. Nonetheless, handling sailing ships, including his large and powerful frigate, was something he understood very well.

Prior to the storm causing *Governor* such problems, *Sabine* had been anchored near Georgetown, South Carolina, as part of the blockade. Bad weather on the morning of November 1st caused Ringgold to weigh anchor and stand out to sea. The big frigate spent the rest of that day and night cruising off shore, waiting for a break in the weather. Sailing in the heavy seas was no doubt uncomfortable, but not dangerous. *Sabine* was still cruising aimlessly waiting out the storm on the morning of the 2d when she came upon a group of ships from Du Pont's scattered fleet. She counted fifteen sail in the forenoon watch alone, proving the ocean a busy highway. Sighting the struggling *Governor* and her two consorts shortly after 1 p.m. Ringgold headed directly for them.

He reached the ships about three o'clock, and "found my worst fears painfully realized. A side wheel steamer, rolling heaving, rudder gone, smokestack overboard, her decks crowded with human beings, lay before me, a helpless wreck..." Although the temperature was warm, the wind was blowing from the south southwest at force seven (about twenty miles an hour), creating dangerously rough seas and leaving Ringgold but a very short time to formulate a workable plan. He described the situation vividly in his report:

> Imagine, sir, the joy that filled our hearts on finding we were just in time to serve and save our countrymen from the jaws of destruction. The helpless condition of the wreck, the imminent peril that environed all, and the fury of the elements left little time for deliberation....The perilous condition of my own ship and the apprehensions for her safety in the event of collision demanded judgment and decision.

Ringgold's plan was simple in concept - to drop *Sabine* back on her anchor line until she lay close enough alongside *Governor* for men to jump from the wrecked steamer to the safety of the frigate.

But more than the turbulent weather and approaching dark made this strategy formidable to execute. Any ship, whether sail or steam, can only maneuver when she is under way so that the thrust of water passing alongside the rudder acts upon it and enables her to maneuver. Without this thrust any vessel becomes as helpless as a log. Thus, for Ringgold's plan to work, he had to position his frigate ahead of *Governor* so precisely that when he anchored and dropped back on his anchor line, *Sabine* would end up close alongside the disabled steamer. Even without the pounding sea this would have been a difficult and delicate task, but after almost eight hours of dangerous and back breaking work, Ringgold's masterly handling of his 1700 ton ship brought her safely into position.

The laconic log of *Sabine* reported tersely:

> At 3:20 lowered a boat & went alongside of her within hailing distance & found she was disabled and had 400 U.S. troops aboard. At 3:50 came to anchor & ran a hawser to the steamer.

As soon as *Sabine* came alongside, around 10 o'clock that evening, the troops aboard *Governor* began the evacuation, leaping through the dark night to the frigate's deck. The already bad conditions worsened as the night wore on; at least twice lines holding the vessels together parted, requiring frantic activity to rig new ones. In the crashing seas and high winds men fell into the sea; six panicked and drowned and one was crushed between the two hulls. *Sabine's* log makes the feat appear quite simple:

> From 6 to 8. Engaged in heaving up anchor and dropping down to steamer *Governor*. Made fast to her and drove her under our stern.
>
> From 8 to midnight. While engaged in assisting the *Governor* added 13 inch hemp line to chain stream cables. She is riding by 3 other hawsers. Let go starb'd anchor, bent port sheet chain to Bower, veered to bitter end of starb'd Bower, which was then shipped & veered to 280 fathoms...Whipped a number of men aboard from the *Governor* and 7 men drowned by jumping overboard.

However Ringgold's florid prose paints a more vivid picture:

[I]n the midst of these operations, at 1 a.m. the gale renewed its fury; the sea which had been gradually subsiding, arose again in all its power, the ship labored at her anchors, and the wreck rolled destructively. As she lurched first to port and then to starboard, burying her sharp bow deep into the trough of the sea, each plunge seemed to be her last...

Here succeeded a scene that beggars description; the despair felt on feeling this attempt at rescue had proved so unsuccessful, the bubbling cry of drowning men, the confusion on board the wreck, the unnatural glare of the sea and sky, caused by the rockets and the red and blue lights...presented a scene that might well have struck terror to the stoutest heart.

Casualties were to be expected but, amazingly, of the four hundred men on the doomed *Governor*, only seven were lost.

By 3:30 in the morning the men on both ships were exhausted. Marine commander Reynolds, aboard *Governor*, advised Ringgold that those remaining could no longer function and suggested suspending further work until daylight. Ringgold concurred and all hands took what rest they could in the few hours before dawn.

Daylight brought a diminishing wind and a clear sky, but the slackened lines between the two ships made impossible the rescue method they had been using. Instead Ringgold sent his only available boat with a crew of his four most experienced men to the wreck. After passing a line to *Governor*, they signaled the men aboard, who jumped into the sea and swam to the boat. This operation continued until 8 a.m. when the vessel was completely evacuated except for Weidman and Reynolds, who began arguing about who was entitled to the "privilege" of being last to leave the wreck. After the contesting officers were hauled safely aboard *Sabine*, Captain Litchfield pulled himself together enough to formally surrender *Governor* to Ringgold.

Not satisfied with his rescue of the *Governor's* company, Ringgold then turned his attention to salvaging their personal effects and whatever public property he could manage to save. He was surprisingly successful, managing to retrieve some 10,000 rounds of ammunition and much of the knapsacks, canteens, and haversacks of the Marines. After his rescue and salvage operations were complete, Ringgold intended to haul off and use *Governor* for target practice. The abandoned ship, however, her pumps now unmanned, sank without any assistance almost at once.

Sabine herself had sustained serious injuries: she had lost two boats, injured her capstan and damaged her rudder, her bowsprit, and her binnacles. Her starboard quarter gallery, which protruded somewhat from the side of the ship, was crushed in and, more seriously, but two reliable sails remained. Worse, with nearly twice the normal number of persons aboard, the water supply was dwindling. Ringgold headed directly for Port Royal and Flag Officer Du Pont, but found himself becalmed. He did not arrive at Port Royal until 8 November.

Ringgold and his crew received the thanks of Congress, a gold medal from the Life-Saving Benevolent Association, and congratulatory resolutions from the Common Council of New York City, and the legislature of the State of Maryland. After sailing to the rescue of the battleship *Vermont* the following spring, Ringgold was promoted to Commodore, but by 1863 both he and *Sabine* were found dispensable. Ringgold spent the rest of the war on shore duty. He was promoted to rear admiral on the retired list in 1866 and died within a year. *Sabine*, like most of the sailing warships, was taken out of commission before the end of the war and never served actively again. She survived her commander by sixteen years, and was sold out of the service in 1883.

The navy did not entirely forget either one, however. It has named two destroyers after Ringgold and at least one oiler after his last command.

CHAPTER IV

Shakedown Cruise

The Ordeal of the *Vermont*

By the end of the War of 1812 the United States Navy enjoyed widespread public acclaim and made plans to increase the fleet by constructing newer, faster and more powerful frigates and ships-of-the-line, the cruisers and battleships of that day. Between 1816 and 1822 the navy laid down the mammoth *Pennsylvania*, 3241 tons and 120 guns, and also nine 74 gun vessels, the prototype of which, *North Carolina*, has been described as "the master ship of the Navy and the world."[1]

Partly due to expense, partly because the enthusiasm of the War of 1812 was cooling, partly because of the inevitable changeover from sail to steam, but probably primarily because they were good "pork barrel" projects (providing work for the party faithful just before elections), construction of these behemoths proceeded at an amazingly slow pace and then very little use was ever made of the ships themselves. Thus *Pennsylvania*, the largest sailing warship ever built in the United States, made her maiden voyage from Philadelphia to Norfolk and was forthwith laid up never to sail again. She was destroyed by fire during the Confederate capture of the Norfolk Navy Yard on 20 April 1861.

The first 74 gun vessel, *Columbus,* was completed in 1819, the only one commissioned as planned. Of the remaining ships, *North Carolina* went into service in 1825, *Delaware* in 1828 and *Ohio* in 1838. The rest of the nine sat unfinished on the stocks until the advent of the Civil War caused the Navy to review their functions and employ them if possible. One of these was the battleship *Vermont,* the only one to actually serve in that or any other war. One hundred ninety-six feet in length, designed to carry a crew of 820 officers and men, and originally intended to carry seventy-four guns, *Vermont* was laid down in Boston in September 1818. Lying on the stocks for more than thirty years before she ever felt salt water, she was left to float untouched for yet another fourteen years until she was finally completed in 1862, not as the imposing ship-of-the-line she was designed to be but as a headquarters and supply ship in the recently captured harbor of Port Royal, South Carolina.

Before she got there, however, Fate had some ordeals in store for her, and she was to make the acquaintance of that windy but expert ship handler, Captain Cadwalader Ringgold and his frigate *Sabine.*

*   *   *

USS *Vermont* went into commission at the Boston Navy Yard on 30 January 1862 with Commander Augustus S. Baldwin in command. It is an indication of the diminished stature of this great ship, originally intended to dominate the seas, that she received as her commander not a senior and veteran captain or the crew of several hundred she was planned for, but a mere commander and a crew of slightly over a hundred and fifty. Baldwin seems to have been regarded as a marginal officer; as a lieutenant he had been transferred to a reserve list in 1856 during a controversial pruning of the Navy list but was resurrected and promoted to commander

USS Vermont, *from a contemporary sketch.*

upon the expansion of the service in 1861. A command of his own gave him an opportunity he must have long coveted.

He did not receive any favors from the navy along the way. For his new and untried forty-year-old ship, he was provided with a crew of 154 officers, warrant officers, marines, seamen and landsmen. Baldwin reported:

> Of those of the crew who had been shipped as ordinary seamen many were boys, one of them only seventeen years old and had never been afloat in his life. Another one informed me that he had not been out of his bed in twelve months until the day previous to his enlistment.[2]

Before any warship, whether she be an old fashioned square rigger like *Vermont* or a modern nuclear submarine, can be effective she must first acquire expertise. Her officers and crew must learn competency in the sailor's skills and then, regardless of their experience, they must learn to employ those skills together as a team and not simply as a collection of individuals. Ideally, as in peace time, the service allows a working up period or shakedown cruise so that the vessel may be proven and the crew learn to function as a team. The exigencies of the crisis denied Baldwin the luxury of such a work up. Instead he was ordered to take *Vermont* to her destination—Port Royal, South Carolina—as soon as she could be made ready to proceed, and he was given a crew barely able to handle her under sail and certainly inadequate to fight her. In compliance with his orders, Baldwin departed from the Boston Navy Yard on 24 February 1862 with sails furled and in tow of the steamer *Kensington.*

The weather—never really good in Massachusetts at that time of year—was very bad, and had the navy possessed our present day knowledge of meteorology, the obsolete square rigger probably would not have been allowed to depart. *Vermont's* problems began even before leaving Boston Harbor. By noon she was able to make sail, but the strong winds almost immediately overpowered her. The untrained and nervous crew were forced to go aloft into the rigging, there to "reef" or tie down part of each sail. By six in the evening, at the height of the gale, the crew had to go up the rigging again to further reduce the sails by double reefing them. An hour and a half later *Vermont* was struck "with a heavy squall from NW which continuing with great force the hawsers [tow lines] were let go by the steamer." Things changed for the worse at once:

> Ship steering very wild. In taking in the mizen topsail it was blown to pieces. Blowing with tremendous sea... Fore and main topsail were blown entirely to pieces. Main sail and spanker blown from the gaskets. Ship low down laboring heavily and making considerable water. Parted fore topmast stay, in setting main topsail carried away the gaff. At 11 PM land was reported on our lee by Commander Baldwin ordered by him to let go both bowers [anchors]... Ship dragging the anchor. At 11:30 PM jib was blown from the gaskets. Gale increasing with great violence Ship entirely unmanageable.
>
> During the night the ship made great quantities of water on the berth deck. So much so as to wash Mess chests and their fastenings and break them into pieces, carrying away the iron Bed cradles in

the sick bay. About 11 PM a port on the starboard side of the sick bay was forced open by which great quantities of water entered destroying entirely the Dispensary and its contents, sweeping away bulkheads, drawers, stove and etc...[S]et gangs of hands at work bailing at which they were employed over 40 hours.

Vermont's unhappy crew endured the storm in the misery of semi-darkness below decks, with the ship pitching and tossing and scattered gear rolling to and fro. To add to their woes, ice, snow, rain and sea water came into the ship, completing their wretchedness. It is true that ships much larger and better equipped than *Vermont* endure great hardships at sea even today, but they are prepared for it with steam power and electric lights.

At 3 o'clock on the morning of February 26 the continuing gale snapped off the ship's iron tiller (six inches square) at the rudder head, and the rudder broke adrift from the ship. With the jib and spanker blown out, the loss of the rudder meant the complete loss of maneuverability. Any vessel under way is normally steered by means of her rudder, a device derived from the ancient steering oar, acting upon the thrust of the water flowing past it. Modern vessels are generally helpless if they lose their rudder, but a square-rigged ship can be steered either with her rudder or by a balancing of wind pressures upon her jibs (the fore and aft sails at the bow) and the spanker (another fore and aft sail running from the mizzen, or after mast); these balance each other and enable the ship to be handled quite readily. With both means of steering gone, the vessel becomes unmanageable and helpless.

The loss of a rudder was not necessarily all that serious. An experienced crew can readily fabricate "jury" or makeshift rigs. Luce's *Seamanship*, the definitive textbook of the time, devotes three times more space to merely tacking, or turning the ship around, than it does to the replacement of a rudder at sea.[3] Baldwin's crew, however, was not experienced.

Drifting in a southeasterly direction from Boston, Baldwin had reason to fear he might be blown onto the beach at Cape Cod, but no one other than Baldwin saw land; if he actually did sight the beach he was fortunate enough to be blown past it without going aground. He was, however, soon drifting across George's Bank, an extensive shallow area about a hundred miles east of Cape Cod, shoaling in places to a mere fifteen feet of water. Since *Vermont* drew twenty-four feet, Baldwin had cause for concern as she drifted across the shoal. But *Vermont* was fortunate: soundings taken at frequent intervals indicated depths of no less than sixty feet.

Late the next morning, 27 February, Baldwin encountered the schooner *Flying Mist,* and sent Acting Assistant Paymaster Edward A. Birnie aboard her to report their predicament to the Navy department. Two days later *Vermont* met the schooner *J. M. Chapman.* Baldwin again forwarded an urgent request for help to the Navy Department:

[U.S.] Ship *Vermont* LAT. 40° 23'N by observation; LONG. by D.R.68° 43'W 43'W March 1, 1862, meridian.

Ship drifting to the S.E. 2 knots, at the mercy of wind and sea. Entirely helpless; rudder and sails gone. Require prompt and powerful steam assistance.

    A.S.Baldwin
    Commander

Both the New York and Boston navy yards, responding to Birnie's pressing telegrams, acted immediately. New York dispatched the gunboat *Dacotah,* the tug *Achilles,* and the steamer *L. Baldwin.* Boston, also concerned about the ship it had dispatched, sent the steamer *Saxon* with a suit of sails, additional tow lines and hawsers, Lieutenant William F. Spicer USN, a boatswain, and a master's mate. It also sent two tugs and the gunboat *Aroostook.*

The day after Baldwin dispatched his appeals by *J. M. Chapman,* *Aroostook* found *Vermont,* restocked her medical supply, stood by her for several days, and attempted to either tow her or help her to turn and get headed westerly. During those five or six days, strong gales blew off *Aroostook's* smokestack and main topmast as well as causing her other damage.

Finally, after nearly two weeks of effort, a tremendous task under the conditions, Baldwin had a new rudder built from the spare timbers carried aboard, and on March 13 it was mounted, enabling *Vermont* to get under way for Port Royal under her own power, at one mile per hour. The sea, however, was not yet ready to let her go. The following day the "hawser sustaining the rudder" was carried away, although, fortunately, it was recovered and repaired. On 15 March, the *Saxon* arrived from Boston with another rudder (taken from one of *Vermont's* unlaunched sisters), the tow was shifted, and the battered *Aroostook* departed.

Baldwin: "Upon Lieutenant Spicer reporting to [me],...I directed him to take the *Vermont* in tow and proceed in a southwesterly direction towards Port Royal, which order he manifested reluctance to obey." Nevertheless, Baldwin's three stripes convinced Spicer's two (or so Baldwin thought) and the tow commenced. However, neither nature nor Spicer would cooperate. "Early on the following morning strong gales....set in..., the tow lines were let go by the *Saxon* and she steamed off out of sight." In an additional indignity, an hour and a half earlier, Baldwin had once again lost his rudder.

On the 17th *Saxon* reappeared but refused to take the line *Vermont* attempted repeatedly to drift to her. Finally she steamed away, leaving *Vermont* and an irate Baldwin in his predicament.

Vermont had yet ten more days to endure her agony before she would find relief, days in which shipping and securing the jury rudder would be impossible. The sails and rigging, which were old and rotten, were continually being split and parting, rain alternated with snow and the winds remained high. Having eluded George's Bank, *Vermont*—still unmanageable—was now approaching Bermuda, several hundred miles southeast of Boston. On 19 March HMS *Landrail* sighted *Vermont* only fifty miles north northwest of Bermuda.

The frigate *Sabine* had sailed in search of *Vermont* on 12 March and by a combination of luck and good navigation found her nearing the dangerous shores of Bermuda on the 28th. The big frigate passed close under the lee of the battered battleship and "greeted her with hearty cheers." Ringgold expected *Vermont* to be in dire straits the worse since "her shattered look and lost rudder too plainly exposed the ravages of the storm" but to his surprise he learned that the battleship was not leaking, that all was well on board and that a jury rudder had been fabricated. By the 30th Ringgold impatiently directed Baldwin to "make every possible exertion" to get the rudder mounted, an order which must have caused Baldwin, who had more interest in mounting the rudder than did Ringgold, to bite his tongue. At any rate, when the winds finally moderated the rudder was mounted, although not without problems, and Baldwin sailed for Port Royal at last.

To the great relief of her crew, the rest of the voyage was routine. Parting company with *Sabine* on 4 April, she had a smooth passage, arriving at the bar off Port Royal on 13 April. However *Vermont* endured one more test before finally entering port. On the morning of the 14th, again in tow of the *Kensington*, *Vermont's* tow line parted and she went aground. Augustus Baldwin would surely have been forgiven if at that moment he had thrown his hat to the deck and jumped up and down on it.

Vermont spent several uncomfortable hours aground. In the afternoon she "made signals of distress and hoisted the ensign upside down and firing guns." Finally she slid off and at 7 p.m. April 14 anchored in Port Royal Sound. The shakedown cruise was over and *Vermont's* greatest days had come and gone with her maiden voyage. She had survived her tribulations intact despite exposure to the vicissitudes of nearly half a century of Massachusetts weather, and despite her untrained crew. *Vermont* spent the rest of the war as a relief command ship for the South Atlantic Blockading Squadron. At war's end she went to New York where she lay at her slip until 1902 when she was broken up, her sister ships long gone, her one great adventure long over, and the age of sail in which she was conceived vanished forever.

Baldwin, who had been given an assignment beyond his capabilities, did not escape unscathed. Relieved of command shortly after his arrival at Port Royal, he spent the rest of the war at a desk job in the Brooklyn Navy Yard. Promoted in 1867 to Captain on the Retired List, he died 1 February 1876 at the end of a loyal and honorable, if not spectacular, career. Many men have done far worse and the crew of *Vermont* had him to thank for their lives.

CHAPTER V

The Battle of Hatteras Inlet

A complete naval blockade of the South would be required to prevent the import of military supplies into the Confederacy and to suppress the irritating numbers of small commerce raiders dashing out of the numerous inlets along the coast, swallowing up Northern merchantmen and scuttling back to the safety of inland waters. Suppression required both formal blockade of the principal seaports and control of the numerous small inlets. Of course, possession of the inlets themselves would be the most complete form of suppression.

Control of the larger seaports, such as Savannah or Charleston, required large scale operations well beyond the power of the Union to mount in the early days of the war. It would be the very last year of the conflict before either of those ports would fall, and they would consume massive amounts of Federal energy before they did. However, it was possible early on in the war to make a beginning at the other points of entry, the numerous relatively uninhabited inlets which stretched along the Confederacy's coastline. At the top of the list of entry areas was Hatteras Inlet on North Carolina's Outer Banks; it was to provide the site of the first combined operation of the war.

*   *   *

Eastern North Carolina is an ecological treasure. Protected from the turbulent waters of the Atlantic by flat and marshy barrier islands, its drowned lands contain two large interconnected bodies of water: Albemarle and Pamlico Sounds. Fed by four big rivers—Chowan, Roanoke, Pamlico and Neuse—they include the cities of New Berne, Edenton and Elizabeth City, from which commerce flowed by rail to the whole South. In 1861 these two sounds were large and deep enough to carry the ocean-going vessels of the time, once they had passed through Hatteras Inlet. The other inlets, Oregon and Ocracoke, were useful for smaller vessels only.

On Hatteras Island at the eastern edge of this inland sea lies Cape Hatteras, known for centuries as the graveyard of the Atlantic, and given as wide a berth as possible by mariners because of its turbulent seas and treacherous shoals. A few miles south of the cape itself is Hatteras Inlet; its broad and relatively deep channel having sufficient depth over the bar to permit passage of vessels of moderate size. This area remains sparsely populated to this day; at the time of the Civil War it was relatively deserted and barren. At the very southern tip of the island, the Confederates had built two forts, one overlooking Pamlico Sound and the other at the edge of the ocean. From this harbor of refuge, they sent small raiders in sufficient numbers to cause annoyance to the North out to prey upon any vessel they saw from the lighthouse.

After questioning several ship captains who had been taken at Hatteras and then permitted to go north, Flag Officer Silas Stringham, commanding the Atlantic Blockading Squadron reported to the Navy Department on 6 August 1861 that Hatteras was "decidedly the worst place on the coast."[1] The next day he reported that there were "two well constructed batteries" there, with six to eight heavy guns with more to follow and a garrison of 300 men. Their methods were described by Lieutenant Thomas O. Selfredge, commanding USS *Cumberland*:

> Hatteras Inlet, a little south of Cape Hatteras light, seems their principal rendezvous. Here they have a fortification that protects

them from assault. A lookout at the lighthouse proclaims the coast clear and a merchantman in sight; they dash out and are back again in a day with their prize. So long as these remain it will be impossible to entirely prevent their depredations, for they do not venture out when men-of-war are in sight; and in the bad weather of the coming season, cruisers can not always keep their stations off these inlets without great risk of going ashore.[2]

One of these released captains related that during the time he was at Hatteras, he saw as many as fifty vessels pass through the inlet, nine as captives, and as many go out bound for Liverpool, Halifax, and the West Indies.[3] This state of affairs clearly invited action from the Navy Department whose response, already in preparation, was to mount the first combined operation of the war.

On 13 August, Major General George B. McClellan, then General in Chief of the army, ordered Major General John E. Wool at Fort Monroe to prepare "a sufficient detachment to accompany an expedition" against the batteries at Hatteras Inlet. Despite the wording of the order it was intended that the expedition be under the control of the navy and under the command of Flag Officer Stringham. Stringham believed otherwise but proceeded to organize it anyway, selecting the naval vessels to participate and chartering merchant vessels to carry the troops.

General Wool designated 200 officers and men from Camp Butler and 600 from Camp Hamilton plus one company of the Second Artillery, all to be under the command of Major General Benjamin F. Butler. Butler was then an unknown factor. An excellent lawyer and politician, he had obtained his commission by political means. Although he was controversial, he had attracted favorable attention in the right places by his peremptory occupation of Baltimore in the touchy early days, when Maryland's status in the Union hung in the balance. For Butler, whose star rose and fell with some regularity during the war, this was to be his finest hour and regardless of the intent of McClellan's order, he intended to get some of the credit.

After some problems with the seaworthiness of the merchantmen, the expedition was ready to go by 23 August, but was delayed by high winds and turbulent seas. By 26 August, however, the weather had moderated and the invasion force departed. The heavy artillery of the force consisted of the flagship *Minnesota*, carrying both Butler and Stringham, together with the steam frigate *Wabash*. These two ships were considered at the time to be two of the most powerful warships in the world. They were accompanied by the steam sloops *Monticello* and *Pawnee* and the gunboat *Harriet Lane*. The troops were carried by the chartered transport steamers *Adelaide* and *George Peabody* and the tug *Fanny*. The transports were towing schooners with surfboats embarked; *Monticello* and *Pawnee* were towing additional boats. The squadron was to be joined during the action by the steam sloop *Susquehanna* and the sail frigate *Cumberland*.

The distance from Hampton Roads, Virginia, to Hatteras is not great; the flotilla arrived and anchored off the inlet in the afternoon of the 27th in sufficient time to permit the hoisting out of surfboats and preparation for the landing of troops in the morning. The flotilla then anchored for the night and made ready for the assault.

The south end of Hatteras Island, as with most barrier islands, is a long sand spit; the shoreline marking the edge of the inlet itself runs parallel to the channel for almost half a mile. Along this shore the Confederates had constructed their two forts: Hatteras on the inside facing Pamlico Sound, and Clark at the eastern edge facing both the sea and the channel. Like many other fortifications erected by the Confederacy, they were not forts in the conventional sense, made of stone or brick, but primarily of sand and sod. Nevertheless they were deemed formidable, and on 25 July Major Bevershaw Thompson CSA, chief engineer of the department of coast defense, believed that the completion of Fort Clark rendered the inlet secure against any attempt of the enemy to enter it.[4] The plan of the operation was not elaborate. The troops would be landed some two miles up the beach from the forts, cutting them off from assistance by land. After the naval vessels had battered the forts into submission, the troops would advance and take them,

The USS Wabash, *in 1861, when she was the pride of the wooden navy. Despite gallant action at Hatteras, and several years of further service, she was superseded as a fighting ship by the new ironclads.*

first Clark and then Hatteras. To accomplish this the plan was for *Wabash*, towing *Cumberland*, and *Minnesota* to approach the coast as near as safety would permit and then steam counterclockwise in a long elliptical pattern, giving full employment to the guns on both sides of the ships. While this was going on, *Monticello, Pawnee* and *Harriet Lane* would escort the troop transports up along the beach, keeping the bombarding vessels between them and the forts.

The plan worked surprisingly well. On the morning of the 18th *Minnesota* fed her crew breakfast early and then sent a 12 pound rifled gun and a 12 pound howitzer to the transport *Adelaide*; and General Butler, together with the ship's marines, shifted to *Harriet Lane*. When this had been accomplished Stringham gave the signal to disembark troops. *Wabash* moved in to take *Cumberland* in tow, while the screening vessels moved forward to protect the transports.

By ten o'clock the pieces were all in place and *Wabash*, still towing *Cumberland*, began the engagement by opening fire on Fort Clark. Not to be outdone, Stringham took big *Minnesota* inside of the two bombarding vessels, temporarily masking them from the enemy's fire, and joined the bombardment. "These vessels continued passing and repassing the fort until it was abandoned by the enemy."[5] During this time the three vessels were joined by *Susquehanna*, and Butler with his troops could now land without enemy interference.

Their disembarkation was not to be easy. The boats used were not designed for the purpose as are today's landing craft; they were regular pulling boats with sharply pointed bows and the only way men could be disembarked was over the side into the water. Getting men ashore safely became difficult in the face of a heavy wind and sea. While conditions were tolerable at the outset, the wind and surf increased as the day wore on, adding to the difficulty of landing the troops. By the time the transports had landed about 300 men, the surf had become so heavy that the boats filled with water, and the landing process had to be interrupted, leaving the assault on the forts to the troops already on shore. They were in no danger, however, because of the efficiency of the fire support of the bombarding vessels, augmented by the fire of those ships assigned to assist the landing force. It turned out that such support was unnecessary.

Prior to this war, it had been axiomatic that warships were simply not capable of standing up against forts. Admiral David D. Porter, for instance, declared that one gun ashore was considered equal to five on shipboard.[6] This may have been true in the days of fighting sail; it was not true in this day's bombardment because of the overpowering superiority of the Union fleet. This barrage, a feeble forerunner of naval bombardments of later wars or, indeed, of this one, lasted just two hours and thirty minutes. To the unfortunate

Confederates in Fort Clark it must have seemed like the commencement of Armageddon.

According to Colonel William C. Martin of the Seventh North Carolina Volunteers, the fort had exhausted its supply of ammunition by noon and it was determined to retire to Fort Hatteras.[7] At 12:25 the flags came down, and the garrison was seen by lookouts aboard *Wabash* to be running towards Fort Hatteras; some were observed leaving the shore in small boats. The way was open for the Federal troops to occupy Fort Clark, which they did by 2 p.m.

Stringham then provided Commander John P. Gillis of *Monticello* with a pilot and ordered him to feel his way into the inlet and try his luck against Fort Hatteras. He took his ship in gingerly, groping between the lines of breakers with the aid of a lead line and striking bottom frequently. Although the pilot took him up the wrong channel, he was able to negotiate the inlet all the way inside to where the channel divided, where he found so little water that he had difficulty in handling his vessel. At this point he was taken under fire by Fort Hatteras and sustained considerable damage, before he was able to turn around and retire to safety. With this, Stringham called a halt to the day's activities and took the squadron offshore for the night, leaving *Monticello*, *Pawnee* and *Harriet Lane* behind to protect the troops. Although reinforced by fresh troops the Confederates made no counterattack on Fort Clark, and were content to await the following day, probably with no great sense of hope.

Daybreak must have been welcome to the Federal troops on shore, however, for the supplies which were to have been landed with them had been left behind in the angry surf; hungry officers were reduced to capturing wild sheep with their swords and roasting them in campfires.[8] The morning brought little relief, however, for the surf was so high that Stringham's order to either provision the troops or embark them[9] could not be complied with. He must not have expected compliance, however, for shortly thereafter he ordered the squadron to open fire on Fort Hatteras, an order made redundant by the fact that *Wabash* had already begun the engagement. The fire delivered by *Wabash* and *Minnesota* was augmented first by *Susquehanna*, then at nine o'clock by *Cumberland* which came in the inlet *under sail*, ("handsomely," as Stringham put it), anchored under *Minnesota's* bow and commenced delivering her fire on the hapless Confederates.

Axiomatic or not, few persons protected only by piles of sand can withstand the concerted fire of heavy artillery delivered at close range; the Confederate garrison was no exception. At 10 a.m. Stringham ordered the squadron to use 15 second "fuzes," a measure certain to demoralize the garrison, now faced with what was the equivalent of shrapnel. At eleven o'clock a white flag was displayed on Fort Hatteras and the inlet was in Union hands. At the sight of this, the troops on shore headed for the fort and took possession, followed closely by their commander, General Butler, who boarded the tug *Fanny*, passed through the inlet and entered the fort personally, where he forthwith rewarded himself by ordering a major general's salute to be fired.

He did not get ashore peacefully, however, and his rashness almost got him into trouble. As *Fanny* approached the inlet, she encountered three steamers and several schooners with enemy troops on board. Despite their threatening aspect, when the brash little *Fanny* fired her rifled cannon at them, that flotilla decamped promptly, leaving Butler with his moment of triumph.

The rest of the day was spent in occupation and consolidation. Stringham ordered the chartered steamers into the inlet to disembark the troops, in company with *Harriet Lane*. This did not prove easy as it might have been because *Lane*, a former deep sea revenue cutter, grounded, first in the inlet and then *in the surf*. Eventually she got off, completed her assignment and went on her way, later to suffer defeat and capture at Galveston, Texas, on 1 January 1863. The finalities were completed that afternoon when Flag Officer Samuel Barron for the Confederate Navy, and Colonels William F. Martin and William S. G. Andrews, commanders of Hatteras and Clark, came aboard *Minnesota* and signed articles of capitulation to Butler and Stringham.

Commander Henry S. Stellwagen of the chartered steamer *Adelaide* lost no time in bypassing Stringham and reported directly to the Secretary of the Navy, Gideon Welles. He stated that there were captured 1000 stand of arms, 25 cannon and 715 prisoners. However, when Stringham arrived at New York with the prisoners he reported their number to be 670. In either case it was a welcome victory to the North, which had been smarting over its defeat at Bull Run earlier that summer.

As soon as the formalities were over and the process of occupation begun, Butler and Stringham, each hastily left the scene and headed north in an undignified scramble to obtain the lion's share of the glory. Stringham took *Minnesota* and the prisoners to New York where they wound up in charge of the army at Governor's Island. Butler went back to Fort Monroe where he awarded himself the credit. This unseemly race undoubtedly lent a bad taste to the affair.

One sailor, J. D. Kraigbaum, a member of a gun crew aboard *Minnesota*, profited from his own mistake. He had allowed a sponger (a rod with a wet sponge at one end to clear a newly fired gun of burning particles) to fall overboard. According to Stringham, "quick as thought he plunged overboard, grasped it, swam up to the port and was helped in by his comrades." In the euphoria which followed victory, Assistant Secretary of the Navy Gustavus V. Fox authorized his promotion to master's mate "if worthy and qualified"[10] Unfortunately for Kraigbaum, his captain, Gershom Van Blunt, did not deem him qualified and declined to recommend him, possibly because the sponger should not have been lost overboard in the first place. However, he did promise to promote him to petty officer if and when a vacancy arose.

Although the original plan had been to try to block the inlet by sinking vessels in the channel, wiser heads prevailed. Hatteras Inlet became the first, and one of the most important, gates of entry into the heartland of the Confederacy. From the date of its capture until the end of the war, Union gunboats roamed Albemarle and Pamlico Sounds at their pleasure,* denying the Confederacy its vitally needed supplies and holding its towns and cities hostages to their will.

Today the forts are gone, absorbed back into the soft sand from which they were created. Their existence is recognized by a historical marker standing about a mile north of the site near the entrance to the ferry connecting Hatteras and Ocracoke Islands. There is absolutely nothing to remind travelers passing the scene of its historical significance; the only occupants today are fishermen and bathers, although from the ferry, the channel where Gillis struggled with *Monticello* and Selfredge took *Cumberland* in under sail, remains clearly distinguishable from the shoals on either side.

*   *   *

The expedition is recounted in *The Official Records of the Union and Confederate Navies in the War of the Rebellion (ORN)*, Series I, Vol. 6, pages 119 *et seq.*

---

* Strictly speaking they did get one tense moment in 1864 when the Confederate ironclad *Albemarle* gave them a hard time, but this was soon resolved when Lieutenant William B. Cushing blew her up one dark night. The sounds were never really in danger except in the minds of some nervous Union officers.

CHAPTER VI

The Navy, the Navy Yard and General Wool

The Norfolk Navy Yard is not in Norfolk, Virginia. It lies across the Elizabeth River just west of Norfolk in Portsmouth. Until after the Civil War, it was not even known as the Portsmouth but as the Gosport Navy Yard, an indication of its ancient connections with the Royal Navy Yard adjacent to Portsmouth, England.

Hub of the maritime operations of the United States Navy, center of its activities in Chesapeake Bay, and filled to overflowing with ships and naval stores, the Yard became the focus of secessionist activities even before Virginia seceded from the Union in the spring of 1861. Its supine abandonment to inferior forces on 20 April 1861 was a sorry chapter in the history of the navy, presenting the South with enormous quantities of materiel of all sorts and costing the Union the services of sorely needed vessels. Thus the steam frigate *Merrimack*, the sloops of war *Germantown* and *Plymouth* and the brig *Dolphin*, all in immediate readiness for sea, were abandoned, set on fire and destroyed. The inoperative receiving ship *Pennsylvania* (the largest wooden warship ever built in the United States), the famous frigate *United States* (which under Stephen Decatur had captured HMS *Macedonian* and added her to the United States Navy), and the frigates *Raritan* and *Columbia* together with the line-of-battle-ship *Delaware* were all scuttled or burned. Although *United States* had been deemed so decayed as to be not worth burning and simply scuttled, she would be raised, made into a school ship by the Confederates and survive all the other vessels.

Merrimack, of course, would be heard from the following year when on 8 March 1862, raised from the dead, rebuilt with a covering of iron and rechristened *Virginia,* she came out of Gosport and attacked the Union fleet off Hampton Roads, where she destroyed USS *Cumberland* and USS *Congress,* only to be fought to a standstill the following day by USS *Monitor.*

*   *   *

In March 1862, Major General George B. McClellan embarked on his first major campaign, moving his Army of the Potomac from a base near Washington D.C. to that portion of southern Virginia known as "The Peninsula," lying between the York and James Rivers. By the time *Virginia* confronted the Federal navy, McClellan and his troops were firmly committed to the Peninsula.

Following *Virginia's* retreat from her stalemated encounter with *Monitor,* the Norfolk-Hampton Roads area witnessed the largest concentration of forces seen until the closing days of the war. With McClellan's army attempting to pin down what would soon be called the Army of Northern Virginia, the Confederate land and naval forces menaced the Federals on two fronts: the James River-Norfolk complex buttressed by the apparently undefeatable *Virginia* and the Confederate army on the Peninsula, confronting McClellan. Between the two jaws of the vise lay the Federal navy. Although vastly superior in numbers, its real strength was *Monitor,* but that vessel was forbidden to engage *Virginia* under all but the most favorable circumstances, lest she be defeated and all the Union forces routed.

The Union did not have a unified command structure. True, the

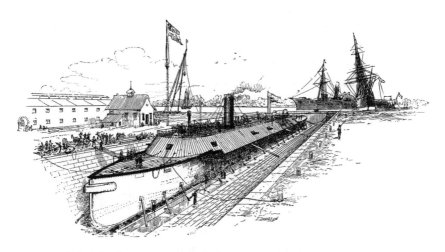

Unusual sketch of USS Merrimack *being covered with armor plate at Gosport to become CSS* Virginia.

navy was under a single commander, Commodore Louis M. Goldsborough, but General McClellan did not command the entire military forces. Commanding what was optimistically labeled the "Department of Virginia" was Major General John E. Wool.

John Ellis Wool was a true anachronism, a relic from bygone days, thrown by chance into a position he was, by reason of age and disposition, incapable of filling. Born in New York in 1784 (older than the constitution he had sworn to protect) he had entered the army as a captain during the War of 1812. Wounded during that conflict, he remained in the service, distinguishing himself in the war with Mexico for which he had been awarded the thanks of Congress, a sword and a brevet promotion.

The outset of the war found him commanding the Department of the East, but he was assigned to the command of the Department of Virginia in August 1861. His principal command was Fort Monroe and its environs, facing Norfolk and the Elizabeth River but protected from the Confederates by the Federal navy. With that considerable force between him and the enemy to the south and with McClellan and the Army of the Potomac between him and the Confederates guarding Richmond, Wool had it as easy as any commander can when he is within ten miles of an armed enemy. To make it easier, he was not expected to do any fighting.

McClellan's siege of Yorktown and his advance towards Richmond began with his arrival at Old Point Comfort (Fort Monroe) on 2 April. As the campaign dragged through the month of April, culminating with the retreat of the Confederates, the Army of the Potomac moved towards Richmond. This advance put great pressure on the Confederates in the Norfolk complex, who began to fancy themselves hopelessly outnumbered and outmaneuvered. Just why they thought so is difficult to fathom. With all of southern Virginia and the northern part of North Carolina in which to maneuver, it is arguable that the invasion of Albemarle and Pamlico Sounds by Brigadier General Ambrose E. Burnside posed no immediate threat to the Norfolk area. Burnside was fully occupied and the consequences of the loss to the Confederacy of the Norfolk complex were so grave that the risk should have been taken. It was, or should have been, clear that McClellan was no threat to Norfolk so long as he was faced by the Army of Northern Virginia; it should have been equally clear that there simply was no Union force available to assault them from the north, either from the Peninsula or from further up Chesapeake Bay.

On the Union side, the navy appears to have been more aggressively oriented; the army leaned towards the defensive. From the outset McClellan was worried over the possibility of *Virginia* destroying his forces. On 12 March he telegraphed Assistant Secretary of the Navy Gustavus V. Fox inquiring whether *Monitor* could keep *Virginia* "in check so that I can make Fort Monroe a base of operations,"[1] and the same day his chief engineer, John G. Barnard, also wired Fox telling him, "The possibility of the *Merrimack* appearing again paralyzes the movements of this army by whatever route is adopted."[2] To these plaintive queries Wool reassured McClellan that *Virginia* posed no threat and Fox backed him up.[3]

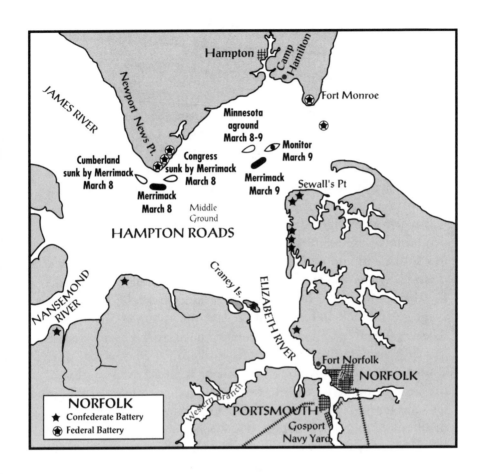

Secretary of the Navy Gideon Welles, who felt the recapture of Norfolk and the navy yard were of prime importance[4], took a more positive attitude than Secretary of War Edwin M. Stanton who, disregarding protocol, involved himself with naval affairs. Stanton telegraphed Cornelius Vanderbilt, the railroad and shipping tycoon who had been active in war preparations, inquiring what would be the cost of sinking *Virginia* or preventing her coming out, a job clearly naval.[5] Confederate Major General Benjamin Huger, commanding the defenses of Norfolk, felt otherwise however. Less than a week after the *Monitor-Virginia* affair, with the Federals still trying to stabilize their forces and making absolutely no threatening noises in the direction of Norfolk, he wrote Judah P. Benjamin, the Secretary of War, telling him that he believed ironclad vessels (the Union had only one in sight) could "pass all our batteries with impunity" and suggesting that the channel out of the Elizabeth River be blocked.[6] Benjamin, one of the most intelligent members of the Confederate hierarchy, saw things more realistically and replied, pointing out that, "None of us are of opinion that it would be proper to lose the vast advantages resulting from the enemy's fright at the bare idea of the *Virginia* reappearing among the wooden ships."[7] The Union leadership, beginning with Secretary of War Stanton, and running all the way down to Commodore Goldsborough, was almost to a man mesmerized by the fearsome thought of *Virginia* clanging down the Elizabeth and destroying the hapless Federals. At the same time, Huger and many like him suffered at the thought of the little *Monitor* storming up the same river and devouring *Virginia* at will.

The stalemate on the Peninsula broke on 4 May when, after almost a month of watching McClellan's leisurely construction of the siege works at Yorktown, the Confederate commander, Major General Joseph E. Johnston, evacuated Yorktown and pulled back in the direction of Richmond. The news acted like a tonic upon President Abraham Lincoln, and he came to Fort Monroe accompanied by Secretary of War Stanton and Secretary of the Treasury Salmon P. Chase.

With the perfect hindsight vision of today, it can be seen that each side in the Norfolk area was equally afraid of the other. In the end it was Huger who blinked and ordered the evacuation of Norfolk. This step, of course, saddled the Confederate navy with the problem of how to dispose of *Virginia*. She could only retreat up the Elizabeth River a very few miles before it dwindled away; she could steal out of the Elizabeth into the James, thence west to help defend Richmond; she could come out in a fiery charge and battle the Federals to the death; she could destroy herself; or, finally, she could ignominiously haul down her colors and surrender. Nobody seriously contemplated the latter.

CSS Virginia *rams USS* Cumberland; *the costliest defeat suffered by the U.S. Navy to that date.*

When steps for the evacuation of Norfolk were observed, Goldsborough brought his forces into action. On the 8th he bombarded Sewall's Point with *Dacotah, Naugatuck, Seminole, Susquehanna* and, significantly, *Monitor.* The ironclad, which had been ordered to avoid conflict with *Virginia,* flaunted herself by joining the attack on Sewall's Point (the site of the present Naval Operating Base). Despite this air of boldness, however, her orders in the event of *Virginia's* appearance were "to fall back into fair channel way , and only to engage her seriously in such a position that [*Minnesota*] could run her down."[8] *Baltimore,* an unarmed steamer of high speed and light draft, was kept close to *Monitor,* prepared to throw herself in front of *Virginia* but her services were not needed as the Confederate ship did not attack.

Virginia did come out as far as Craney Island early on the morning of the 10th but, while threatening, once more failed to attack. The activities of these two days, however, convinced General Wool at Fort Monroe that the time to attack Norfolk was at hand, and preparations were made for the landing of troops. These were encouraged by Lincoln who, together with Chase, had toured the naval force and observed the obvious weakness of the defenses at Sewall's Point.

Wool's forces landed at Sewall's Point on the 10th and headed for Norfolk. He, himself, arrived there about five in the afternoon and took the surrender of the mayor and city council.[9] Wool claimed he had taken possession of Gosport and Portsmouth, but he could not have been serious about it because the navy yard was still in the possession of the Confederates.

Despite the apparent completeness of the victory, Wool, apparently more pleased by his receiving the surrender of the town than by the necessity of holding it, neglected to order up reinforcements, a neglect which earned him the wrath of the President of the United States. Lincoln, back at Fort Monroe after his naval excursion, saw for himself Wool's failure to procure reinforcements. Sending for Brigadier General Joseph K.F. Mansfield, commanding Ohio troops, and Colonel Joseph B. Carr, commanding the 2d, 9th and 10th New York and the 9th Massachusetts, he inquired why they and their troops had not crossed over to Norfolk. Upon being informed by Mansfield that he had been ordered to the fort and by Carr that he was "awaiting orders," Lincoln, for once, lost his temper. Throwing his well known tall hat vehemently on the floor and venting his feelings strongly and audibly he dictated an order to Wool directing that the troops then at Camp Hamilton be immediately ordered to Norfolk and that the troops already there be pushed rapidly forward.[10]

Wool's tardiness had given the Confederates the time they needed to destroy the navy yard (for a second time) and dispose of

Virginia. They worked all night doing so. It had originally been decided to take the ironclad down the Elizabeth and up the James to aid in the defense of Richmond. To this plan, the ship's pilots, upon whose services the vessel was absolutely dependent for navigation of the river, raised all sorts of objections that seem designed to ensure failure. First they laid down all sorts of objections: that the run must be made in daylight; that there was no harbor of refuge in the event of a storm; that the removal of buoys and other aids to navigation made their task difficult if not impossible; and that the deep draft of the vessel made it impossible for her to ascend the river. Most of these objections could be overcome by the forceful and dynamic leadership of *Virginia*'s commander, Captain Josiah Tattnall, who had already proven his ability. The problem of her deep draft, however, had but one solution: the removal of her armor and other weights to lessen her draft.

To this end the Confederates worked feverishly, succeeding in reducing her draft to the required limit; whereupon the pilots then declared that the west wind had blown the water out of the river,[11] lowering the water level, and she could not complete the voyage under any circumstances. This claim is very suspicious; *Dacotah*'s log records the wind on 8 May as "light easterly" and on 9 May as west, force 2, a gentle breeze. At any rate Tattnall was in a dilemma; he had irrevocably destroyed his ship's invulnerability by throwing off her armor, and his pilots had declared she could not be taken to safety. Since she could neither fight nor flee and since surrender was unthinkable, destruction was the only route left. In a sorry ending for one of the most noteworthy of American naval vessels, North or South, early on the morning of 11 May the beleaguered *Virginia*, progenitor of all modern surface warships, was driven ashore in the vicinity of Craney Island, abandoned by her crew, and set on fire. After about an hour came the inevitable ending, obvious to all from the vehemence of the explosion.

Considering the implications arising from the elimination of so formidable an adversary, the Union vessels treated it in their logs in a casual manner. *Dacotah*'s log, for example merely states,

"Another fire opening up bearing SSW caused by the rebel steamer *Merrimack*. At 4.55 Rebel steamer *Merrimack* blew up." *Susquehanna* merely reported, "At 5, an explosion was heard in direction of Craney Island." *San Jacinto* was less terse: "At 4.55 a.m. heard the report of a great explosion in the direction of Craney Island. Immediately after, the flag ship hoisted No. 5 & fired a gun. The crew were instantly beat to quarters and this ship put in an efficient state for action & anchor ready for slipping." Goldsborough knew the import of the explosion. Shortly after six o'clock, as soon as it was light enough to move safely, he ordered *Dacotah*, *Susquehanna*, *San Jacinto*, *Seminole*, and *Naugatuck* to advance towards Norfolk. To protect them, he ordered *Monitor* to accompany them, the first time ever that the doughty vessel had been ordered to advance towards *Virginia*, and proof positive that Goldsborough understood his formidable adversary was no longer a threat.

Tattnall, with his consent, was given a general court martial. The court found that he was in no way to blame for the loss of *Virginia* but that, to the contrary, "the only alternative...was to abandon and burn the ship which, in the judgment of the court, was deliberately and wisely done by order of the accused."[12] This decision is certainly justifiable but it is significant that one of the members of that court was Captain Franklin Buchanan, *Virginia*'s first commander. Two years later, by then an admiral, Franklin Buchanan was placed in a similar situation at Mobile Bay, Alabama. Aboard *Tennessee*, the last of the great Confederate ironclads, he faced Rear Admiral David G. Farragut and a host of Federal warships including ironclads. Pausing only long enough to regroup, he charged into the entire Union fleet in a determination to go down fighting. While Farragut is reported to have said, "I did not think that Old Buck was such a fool," the likelihood is that both of them were thinking of the fate of Tattnall and the unfortunate *Virginia*.)

The advance up the Elizabeth was not entirely an easy expedition. The Confederates had long since cluttered the channel with wrecks and obstructions although they could not completely close

The historic confrontation of USS Monitor *and CSS* Virginia *(ex-*Merri-mack*)*

it in order to permit *Virginia* and her consorts to come out and harass the Federals. Still, they did a reasonably thorough job; *Dacotah* "went carefully up Elizabeth River through the obstructions. Ship scraped over a sunken wreck alongside the frigate *United States.*" While *Dacotah* may have "scraped over the wreck," *San Jacinto* was not so lucky. After passing Craney Island at 9:30, she "Got ashore in the middle of the channel. On top of a sunken wreck placed there by the rebels to obstruct the channel tried to back off with the assistance of a towboat, but of no avail." She remained on top of the obstruction until 2:30 p.m., when she "got afloat" and went on up the river, anchoring abreast of Norfolk at 3:15. However *San Jacinto's* time on the wreck was not wasted, because, during the time she was aground she occupied herself by sending a boat ashore "to take possession of a large battery."

Susquehanna, after obtaining a pilot from *San Jacinto* (which may explain why that pilotless vessel got aground) "passed pieces of a wreck supposed to be that of the ~~Confederate~~ Rebel'str *Merrimac*" was halted by piles driven to obstruct the channel. Luckier than her consort, she "steamed ahead strong & passed over them" as did all the other vessels. Both she and *Dacotah* reported passing by the hulk of *United States*. When *Susquehanna* came to anchor off Norfolk at 11:00 the Union flag was flying over the Custom House and the Naval Hospital. At 11:30 Goldsborough came aboard and hoisted his flag, and the occupation of Norfolk and the navy yard was to all intents complete. Whose occupation it was, however, was not entirely clear except to Wool. His report of May 12[13] makes it crystal clear that, in his eyes, it was he and he alone who took the city. He appears to have done his best to get in conflict with the navy. He was at least consistent in his exercise of authority; he had, for instance, earlier on, interfered with the assignment of a naval officer[14] and had been stuffy over a proposed transfer of an island in Hampton Roads called the Rip Raps from the army to the navy.[15] He was now to demonstrate his inability to work with anybody except on his own terms.

On 21 May Secretary Welles advised Goldsborough that he was sending down a battalion of Marines for duty at the navy yard and ordered him to confer with Wool "with regard to delivering up the navy yard." The "conference" was one sided. To Goldsborough's not unreasonable request Wool stuffily responded:

> I would remark that Fort Norfolk was surrendered to the troops under my command on the 9th instant by the rebels of Norfolk. I can not therefore permit the Navy to take possession of it without an order from the President of the United States or the Secretary of War.

And in prompt answer to Goldsborough's request that, since

---

* An illustration of the reluctance of the Navy Department to use the term "Confederate" lest it legitimize the rebellion.

John Ericsson, designer of the USS Monitor. *He was foreign-born (in Sweden), as were one out of every four Civil War participants. Lumber rafts in his native country may have inspired* Monitor's *design.*

they were already on the way, the Marines at least be allowed to land until the matter was straightened out, Wool wrote back:

> I can not permit the Navy to take possession of any of the works, including the navy yard or depot, in the vicinity of Norfolk, all having been surrendered to me and taken possession of by the troops under my command, without the authority of the President of the United States or the Secretary of War.

The most obvious immediate solution to this impasse was to go through channels. This Welles did, obtaining an order from Stanton to Wool, directing him to turn the yard over to Goldsborough. Even then Wool refused to be gracious, merely writing to Goldsborough "authorizing" him to take possession.

Wool was not finished, however. The Yard and channel were littered with wrecks, many of them of vessels belonging to the navy;

Goldsborough was directed by Welles to commence the process of raising them both for salvage and for clearing of the channel. It was learned on 26 May that the enterprising Wool had already entered into contracts for the raising of the sunken vessels, including the wreck of *Virginia,* and had taken the position that he had been required to turn over only the property at Gosport and not any other navy property in the area. This required more paper work to clear the air.

Wool would not give up on *Virginia's* bones. On 1 June he wrote to Goldsborough:

> Before the property belonging to the Navy was ordered to be turned over to the navy agents I made a contract to raise the *Merrimack.* The contractor had already commenced when you gave orders to those engaged in it not to interfere with the raising. This vessel does not belong to the Navy, she being entirely remodeled and ironclad at the time of her destruction. If there should be found any timbers remaining that would be serviceable to the Navy they will be turned over to the Navy. I have therefore to request that you will not again interfere with the raising of the wreck. I will see that the public interest is protected.

Goldsborough pointed out that the wreck "is placed distinctly under my charge by the Navy Department, and as to your statement about her not belonging to the Navy, I differ with you entirely in opinion."

It must have seemed clear to every one concerned that Wool simply did not possess the least concept of inter-service cooperation and certainly his delay in bringing up reinforcements to Norfolk had not endeared him to President Lincoln. The replacement of Wool ended the turmoil. On 1 June Major General John A. Dix was ordered to replace him, and when Dix protested to Stanton that he regarded such a post as "a degradation" he was advised by the secretary:

> The change of your command was determined by the President himself. The order was prepared by his direction in my absence, I

did not advert to the effect of it, but know that nothing could have been further from the President's purpose than to displease, much less offend you.

What remained to be done was the long, slow process of cleaning up the Yard, the channel and the river. Of the wrecks, only that of *United States* was serviceable, although she had been so neglected prior to the war that she had only been used by the Confederates as a school and barracks ship. By the returning Federals she was not used at all. She was broken up shortly after the war, with tales still remaining about the legendary hardness of her live oak timbers in spite of her years of neglect. How much of *Virginia* was raised is not disclosed; the likelihood is that most of her still lies under the mud of a now greatly expanded Craney Island.

CHAPTER VII

A Friday Sailing: The Misadventures of the *Wabash*

Governor, *Vermont* and *Passaic* were all victims of the sea's fury, of the weather and not the enemy's fire. The same is true of USS *Wabash* except that she had an additional drawback–it was Friday. Sailors are perhaps among the most superstitious of all humans, and of all superstitions, one of the most prevalent is that an Friday sailing will prove disastrous. Sailors have been known to resort to ingenious devices to avoid a Friday departure and, when unavoidable, to seize upon the slightest calamity as proof of the belief's validity.

USS *Wabash* was a distinguished vessel. One of a class of five steam frigates built by the Federal Navy just before the Civil War,[1] she was a screw steamer of 4650 tons carrying a crew of 550. Mounting one 150 pound Parrott rifle and forty-two 10 inch Dahlgren smooth bore guns, she has been called one of "the most powerful warships in the world."[2] Useless for inshore blockading because of her size and deep draft, she nevertheless participated in fleet actions from the attack on Hatteras in August 1861 to the final assault on Fort Fisher in January 1865. She was utilized primarily as a flagship, most of the time at Port Royal, South Carolina, where she was in October 1864, under the command of Captain John DeCamp.

*   *   *

Captain John DeCamp was no stranger to naval warfare; as a commander he had directed *Iroquois* in 1862 when she fought her way past Forts St. Philip and Jackson in the Mississippi River, and Admiral Farragut had recommended that he receive the thanks of Congress for this feat. Transferred from *Iroquois* to the gunboat *Wissahickon* following the capture of New Orleans shortly thereafter, DeCamp took her against the Confederate batteries at Grand Gulf, Mississippi, which shot her up badly, and thence up the Mississippi to Vicksburg where she once more received serious damage. During this latter engagement, DeCamp, although confined to his bed with yellow fever, took the deck to set an example for his crew. As a reward for his actions, he now found himself captain of *Wabash*, the flagship of the South Atlantic Blockading Squadron.

The duties of a flagship stationed in a remote harbor and rarely going to sea are hardly exciting. Remaining constantly at anchor at Port Royal, the crew was occupied more with spit and polish than with training for sea duty and they must have received gratefully the news that *Wabash* was to be relieved and proceed to Norfolk, Virginia, for liberty and an overhaul. However, had they foreseen the adventures that lay between Port Royal and Norfolk, they well might have protested beginning the voyage on a Friday. At 4:20 on the afternoon of Thursday, 29 September 1864, *Wabash* fired a thirteen gun salute to the flag officer, went out into the harbor and anchored to await a tide which would permit her to cross the bar.

Her choice of anchorage was unfortunate. At 1:15 in the morning of Friday the 30th, the ship, "swinging to the flood tide touched on the Western bank of the channel." At 2:00 she again touched, whereupon DeCamp started the engine to keep her clear of the shoal. At 5:50 a.m. *Wabash* weighed anchor, crossed the bar, and commenced her journey to Norfolk.

Despite the inauspicious beginning in the harbor, the first day at sea went well and *Wabash* steamed at a moderate pace up the

South Carolina coast. At 5 p.m. she sighted the Charleston block-ading fleet and at 8 p.m. observed the Charleston lightship bearing southwest by south at a distance of twenty miles. At the same time she sounded and found ten to twelve fathoms of water. That night was also routine. Soundings taken at frequent intervals disclosed eight to ten fathoms, and the last, just before noon on 1 October, showing twelve fathoms.

The forenoon watch was uneventful. *Wabash* steamed generally northeast at five to six knots in light airs, until 9 a.m. when the course was changed to Northeast by East. Soundings taken at 11:30 disclosed twelve fathoms. In the afternoon watch the log records:"At 12 the color of the water changes to lighter green. At 1:30 the water shoaled to 6 1/2 fathoms. Slowed down. At 1:30 1/2 [the ship] went ashore in 3 1/4 fathoms fwd and quarter less 4 aft. Brailed [furled] up fore and aft sails and backed the engine."[3] *Wabash* had gone aground on Frying Pan Shoals.

Extending several miles in a Southwestwardly direction from Cape Fear, at the mouth of the Cape Fear River, in which lay the port of Wilmington, North Carolina, Frying Pan Shoals were (and still are) a menace to navigation. Their extensive size and extreme shallowness made them a genuine impediment to the Federal blockade of Wilmington, as well as a trap for the unfortunate mariner who failed to keep an accurate track of his position.

According to DeCamp the ship "struck moderately" and was able to stop at once, since her speed at the time was not "much more than 4 knots." Her log, however, reports she was doing six—half again as much—that much additional momentum for the heavy *Wabash*.

When the ship went aground, the executive officer, Lieutenant Elliott C. Blake, took charge of the deck. A boat was lowered and soundings disclosed eighteen to nineteen feet from the bow to amidships and five fathoms (thirty feet) on the starboard quarter. All the other boats were then lowered and Blake took charge of them, while DeCamp took the unusual step of by-passing *Wabash*'s officers and leaving the deck watch in charge of Commander

George M. Colvocoresses. Although a passenger, he was undoubtedly qualified for the job. Under Blake's supervision an anchor was carried off the starboard quarter, but with no success. The ensign was then hoisted upside down at the main and fore royal mastheads, signal guns were fired, and at 3:30 Acting Ensign Henry E. Chase was dispatched in a cutter to the Wilmington Blockading Squadron "with orders to state the condition of the ship & ask for assistance." We know the cutter passed the steamer *Eolus,* which arrived on the scene at 6:30, for when her captain came on board, he reported speaking to the cutter "standing for the Wilmington Blockade." No further mention is made of the cutter or her crew, and it appears to have been left behind when *Wabash* went on her way.

Wabash had struck almost at dead low water for, shortly after *Eolus* arrived, the tide was rising rapidly and "at 7 bells the tide acting on the starboard side, the ship slice off [slid] and swung stern to tide." The rising tide combined with the sea caused *Wabash* to strike the bottom "uncomfortably" for the first hour.

The grounding was more serious than the temporary inconvenience DeCamp reported.[4] When *Wabash* eventually arrived at Norfolk, the rudder braces were broken. The sudden stop had also produced pandemonium, judging from conflicting entries in her deck log. Deck logs of that period were written up in printed books furnished by the Navy Department, the pages consisting of printed forms for entering navigational data with some space for narrative. The officer of the deck of each successive watch signed the entry and rarely, if ever, did the commanding officer sign the log. *Wabash's* log entries for the 30th, however, are quite extraordinary. Commencing at noon, one entry covers the entire rest of the day and appears to have been written by Lt. Blake. The scrivener becomes increasingly agitated as the entry continues, and the log concludes with the following bizarre entry:

> Whilst getting out the anchor, the spare spars (mizen chains) were cut adrift and chests and contents, and some light things about

deck, were thrown overboard by whose orders the undersigned is ignorant.

E.C. BLAKE
Lieutenant and Executive Officer.

Immediately below it in DeCamp's handwriting appears the entry:

Remarks: No observation was had this day. supposed the ship to be 23 miles clear of the Frying Pan Shoals, steaming at the rate of 4 knots with fore and aft sails set water 12 fathoms. At 1:20 ship grounded. Got afloat at high water at about 7 p.m. I ordered the solid shot from after locker thrown overboard also the spares from chains. During Lt. Blake's absence from the ship I directed Commander Colvocoresses, passenger to take charge of the deck. Nothing was thrown overboard by my order except the above named items.

J. DeCamp, Captain.

What was thrown overboard is not clear, but enough gear must have been jettisoned to cause comment and justify the above remarks. The guns were not jettisoned although they were buoyed in preparation for going overboard.

On the left hand page in the box where entries for distance covered, latitude, and longitude are to be made, appears the following entry, again in DeCamp's handwriting: "Note—The ship floated clear of the shoal *before* the 'Eolus' came to us: her Captain came on board and rendered me valuable assistance with his advice. John De Camp, Captain."

Wabash spent several hours hoisting boats aboard and cleaning up the decks. At 11:30 p.m. the carpenter's mate reported the ship making water fast from the leakage of the boiler, so she proceeded with extreme caution to Norfolk. For the duration of the trip, a tense and nervous crew took soundings every watch and kept speed at a minimum. With a sense of relief she came to anchor off Fortress Monroe at 1:30 p.m. on Wednesday, 5 October, where she lay until the afternoon of Saturday, 8 October. On that day she got under way for the Norfolk Navy Yard (then known as the Gosport Navy Yard), eight or ten miles straight up the Elizabeth River. In smooth waters on a straight course of that short distance, DeCamp must have felt nothing else could happen to him.

But, as he was heading for Norfolk, however, Commander Edmund R. Colhoun on USS *Saugus,* a 225-foot monitor, agreed to a race from Norfolk Navy Yard to Hampton Roads and back between *Saugus* and her sister ship, the name ship of the class, *Canonicus.* The race almost assuredly lacked the sanction of higher authority. The Newport News-Hampton Roads-Norfolk complex was then, as it is now, the largest concentration of naval forces on the continent. Although the course was straight, the channel was comparatively narrow; the thought of two clumsy monsters like *Saugus* and *Canonicus* thrashing at full speed down the crowded fairway under those conditions is indeed awe inspiring. Nevertheless, they did—and *Wabash* and *Saugus* collided.

Not surprisingly, the two vessels' versions of the accident vary. *Wabash* records that *Saugus* struck her; *Saugus* tells a different story:

> At 1130 hove up anchor and steamed down river in company with *Canonicus.* At 12 meridian started side by side with *Canonicus* on a race down river.... Steamed down to Hampton Roads a distance of 12 miles, *Canonicus* leading. Put about with *Canonicus* right abreast and kept the proceeding, arriving at starting point together at 3 pm. Was run into by U.S.S. *Wabash* having our cutter stove in and sustaining other damage.[5]

No disciplinary action was ever taken against DeCamp. Six months later *Saugus* was involved in another collision, this time with U.S.S. *Baltimore.* While the explanation may lie in the difficulty of handling those iron monsters, this, in turn, points up the foolhardiness of the race in the first place.

Regardless of the blame and despite *Wabash's* escape from damage, she went aground again and spent the weekend "on the flats." One can only imagine the state of mind of her crew—departure on a Friday, half a day on Frying Pan Shoal, a collision, and now ignominious isolation over the weekend in the mud and right in front of the Navy Yard.

Apparently DeCamp employed the same tactic used by the fictitious Commander Queeg of *The Caine Mutiny* fame of World War II. He failed to send in a report of the grounding. Admiral David D. Porter, however, aboard his flagship *Malvern* at Hampton Roads, was bound to learn of so conspicuous a gaffe. As a matter of fact, he received a report from the Navy Department and forthwith called for a report from DeCamp.

DeCamp's report was a model of circumspection, giving only the barest facts. It blamed the Frying Pan Shoals incident squarely on defective compasses (although *Wabash*'s log is conspicuously silent on this subject). The day after submitting this report, De-Camp was relieved of his command and sent to the Philadelphia Navy Yard for a physical examination. In his defense, earlier in the war he had served well and honorably both in and out of combat. Bearing in mind his conduct at Vicksburg when he took the deck suffering from yellow fever, during this voyage he must have been again a sick man. Although he passed the physical examination, he never again served actively at sea, his last command being that of the storeship *Potomac* at Pensacola, in 1865. He was promoted commodore in 1868 and rear admiral on the retired list in 1870. He died in 1875 leaving a record of which he and his descendants might justly be proud. Now, if only he had sailed on a Wednesday....

CHAPTER VIII

Life on the *Maria A. Wood*

The Union Navy's goal during the Civil War was the blockade of the Confederate coast and the strangling of its commerce. Far less glamorous than the breathtaking adventures of the War of 1812 against Britain, then the world's most powerful maritime power, the slow and infinitely tedious naval blockade eventually robbed the Confederacy of her vitally needed supplies and made it impossible for her to supply her grimly tenacious armies.

The blockade was difficult and dangerous, requiring constant vigil. Nevertheless, the greatest enemy was monotony. Historical fiction is full of tales of the British Navy during the Napoleonic Wars, but almost all concern the exploits of Britain's frigate captains, not the blockading fleets which eventually brought down Napoleon. No one has yet been able to romanticize them. Nor, in all that has been written about the Civil War, has anyone yet been able to glamorize naval life in the sounds of North Carolina or Mississippi. The case of USS *Maria A. Wood* is a good example.

*   *   *

Maria A. Wood was a 344 ton schooner, blockading the coasts of Mississippi and Louisiana. Her routine is typical of the average small blockading vessel, except that her captain disappeared, was later found murdered, and became unjustly accused of treason by no less a person than Rear Admiral David G. Farragut, one of that doughty officer's few mistakes.

Maria's log relates that she was commissioned "lying in the stream," presumably at anchor in the river, and not at a pier, at the Philadelphia navy yard on 19 November 1861. She was then given her armament—two 32 pounder cannon reminiscent of the War of 1812. The official records tell us that she was purchased at Philadelphia at a cost of $18,000 and that the total cost of repairs during her service was $15,546.25. But mere accounting tells nothing either of the ship or her crew. All we know is that under the command of Acting Master Anthony Chase and three master's mates, *Maria* went to war just two days later, a new ship with a green crew. We must look to her log for what details we can learn.

Her maiden voyage was as tedious as her service was to be. Her first day's run took her down to Fort Mifflin, some seven miles away. She took three full days to go the eighty miles from Fort Mifflin to Cape Henlopen at the mouth of the Delaware Bay. Chase, with no experienced officer to help him, tried to get the crew in shape on the voyage from Key West to Fort Pickens, Florida, but he had to deal with unruliness as well as inexperience: "John Burnes, boatswain's mate put in irons and disrated grog stopped until further orders from the Capt." Finally, three weeks after setting out, on 14 December *Maria* arrived at Fort Pickens, blockading Pensacola, Florida, and reported to Flag Officer William W. McKean for duty.

Once at Fort Pickens, the shoddiness of her fitting out came to light:

> I feel it my duty to bring to your notice the fact that the *Maria A. Wood* was sent out with three master's mates, neither of whom can work a day's work or take a meridian observation of the sun, and one of them is ignorant of the multiplication table.[1] Had anything happened to the acting master in command there was no one on board capable of navigating the vessel into port. I will also state that she was unprovided passing boxes for powder, that her magazine is not lined, and that the cylinders are put up in rough

pine boxes, fastened with iron nails. Her commander also informs me that he was furnished at the Navy Yard with one old ensign, which, by the time he reached Key West, was completely worn out...Neither of the schooners is supplied with signals of any kind, and I have not a yard of bunting in the squadron.[2]

In this pathetic state of unreadiness, common in the navy in the early days of the war, *Maria* took up her duties as a blockader in the Gulf of Mexico. Most of the time her station ran from Pensacola, Florida, westward to beyond Pascagoula, Mississippi, including the islands of Petit Bois and Santa Rosa, off shore from Pascagoula—as monotonous a beat as could be found anywhere in the war.

Considering that *Maria* had arrived at Fort Pickens unsupplied with signals herself, it seems downright impertinent that on 8 January 1862 she fired on USS *Kingfisher* for not having signals. Someone aboard must have been embarrassed; the log does not reveal that *Kingfisher* was a naval vessel (which she, in fact, was), but describes her merely as "the bark *Kingfisher.*"

Maria's disciplinary problems continued. The log records numerous punishments for infractions of discipline, most probably reflecting the monotony and boredom of the blockade routine. These men were not conscripts; they were volunteers and the service had not yet learned that enlisted men function better when properly informed; no doubt the men on the job could not see how their monotonous routine was winning the war. On January 9 Henry Jensen and another seaman were put in irons "for bad conduct and bad answers." On 27 January "At 8:30 p.m. H.F. Jensen struck boatswain's mate and boatswain's mate disrated to seaman." (Striking a petty officer seems an odd way to bring about his disrating!)

Petty officers were more of a problem to Chase than his nonrated men. On 22 May, "While making sail on the vessel William Dover, Q Mas. [Quartermaster] disobeyed the orders of the officer of the deck and came running up to him with both fists and struck him and began to make use of abusive language to him and at 12 o'clock the Capt. came on board and Dover was put in irons." This intriguing entry sparks all sorts of questions: Why was the vessel making sail—the act of hoisting the sails so as to place the ship in motion—in the absence of the Captain? Why was Dover never disrated if not court martialled? Whatever the answers, Acting Master Chase had his problems.

Possibly the most bizarre incident occurred on 13 March 1863: "At 9:30 the Capt...and Ex. Officer F.C. Way went to Pensacola....At 6:45 the Capt. and Ex. Officer F.C. Way returned on board... At 7:15 put Ex. Officer F.C. Way under restraint and in irons by his own request." Mate [Master's Mate] Francis Way was dismissed from the service on 18 January 1864. We can only speculate on the nature of the problem that led him to request his own confinement.

On 26 January *Maria* anchored at the east end of Santa Rosa Island. There she lay for the better part of the long, dreary winter, often buffeted by storms: "Heavy squalls from the S by W. Schooner roaling heavy... Roaling both guns under." On 17 March hostilities broke the monotony:

> Our boat was in St. Rose's Bay reconnoitering and was attacked by a schooner and a sloop and two of our men was killed. At 8:30 put the corps in a boat and started for the island to berry them but as we approached near the island we saw three small schooners in behind the island laying at anchor and saw some men on the island so we returned with the corps and berried them at sea.

A happier event varied the routine when on 21 March *Maria* rescued eighteen men and a child "which had been at sea 6 days" and took them to Fort Pickens. However, most of the time she lolled at anchor, often rolling heavily.

In spite of the tedium, the break in the routine on 6 April was not a welcome relief: "Saw a suspicious looking schooner bearing SE about 8 miles. The wind being too light to get the ship under way we had 2 boats manned and left the ship...and when they got to within a mile of her a breeze sprung forth and after a chase of 3 hours she got away from them." The long and weary return trip, unmentioned in the log, could not have been a pleasure.

On 12 May 1862, *Maria* made her unique contribution to Union success. Her crew raised the Union flag over Pensacola:

> At 6:15 the troops from the Fort arrived and at 6:15 the Capt. and Executive Officer & Lieut. Koufin (USA) went ashore and took our men and the soldiers that we had on board and they fell in the square around the flagstaff with the troops and at 6:20 two of our crew hoisted the flag and the troops took possession of the city.

For this exploit Brigadier General L. G. Arnold gave her one of her few commendations:

> I take pleasure in adding that the U.S.schooner *Maria A. Wood*, Anthony Chase Master, (U. S. Navy) commanding, was the first vessel that had the honor to run into the harbor of Pensacola...He, with her officers and crew, participated with much speed in reeving new halliards on the flagstaff and running up the flag.[3]

The crew's elation let down three days later when "At 3:30 Pilot ran the vessel aground on an oyster bed 15 miles above Pensacola City." It took twenty-seven hours to get her off.

To break the wearisome routine, the crew took numerous trips to shore, usually to one of the islands nearby. Thus on 4 November 1862 a boat went on shore at Petit Bois Island, off the coast of Mississippi, to search for cattle. Apparently there were none, for in the evening it returned with 2 "boares." While most of the expeditions were for hunting and fishing, the log does record various instances of Captain Chase leaving the ship, sometimes on official business and many times on personal business. One of these expeditions brought real trouble to *Maria* and earned her a sinister niche in history. It also demonstrated the injustice of rumor.

On 21 November Chase, accompanied by an acting master's mate and four armed seamen, left the ship in a cutter to reconnoiter the coast in the neighborhood of Pascagoula, Mississippi. When they failed to return in the evening, Executive Officer Way began to worry:

> Capt, had not returned. I am greatly worried about him. At 5:40 hoisted my ensign and dist[ress] penn[ant] at the main topmast head and fired a gun for the *Jackson*. She came over to us at 6:30 and I sent a boat aboard with the tidings. Capt. Anderson sent for me. I went aboard and explained things just as they were. He thinks he is taken prisoner.

Two days later, the boat still had not returned. The senior officer on the blockade, Captain Thornton A. Jenkins, sent USS *Hatteras* by and her commander placed Acting Master Samuel C. Cruse in command of *Maria* "until the return of her commander or relieved by competent authority." Placing a strange officer in command instead of leaving Way in temporary charge seems to indicate Jenkins's lack of confidence in Way. After ordering Cruse to take command of *Maria*, Jenkins advised his superior, Admiral David G. Farragut:

> Acting Master Anthony Chase, late in command of the U.S. schooner *Maria A. Wood*...left his vessel on the morning of the 21st..in a boat partially armed with an acting master's mate and four men, and stood in the direction of Pascagoula, a distance of about 9 miles, and that no tidings have been received of the boat since she was seen near the long wharf in front of the large hotel at Pascagoula. There seems to be something very suspicious in this business.

After this report rumors began to mount. On 4 December Farragut added fuel to the fire, advising Secretary of the Navy Gideon Welles, "Lieutenant-Commander Madigan reports to me that Acting Master Chase was dressed in citizen's clothes, and also that he had all his money with him."

This report went forward despite Way's report of 22 November that Chase had stated he would not be away for more than an hour or so, that he took no provisions with him, and that Way was "very sure he had no intention of landing, for supposed reasons of my own."

Evidence of Chases's fate began to surface in December. On the 21st, Farragut advised the Navy Department that the body of Charles Bigsby, one of the crew of the missing boat, had been found. Then on the 30th a detail from USS *John P. Jackson* found and buried the bodies of Captain Chase and Jacob Kickline, one of the boat's crew on the north shore of Petit Bois Island. *Jackson* reported, "everything indicates that there was a terrific struggle on the part of the boat's crew."

Rumors still persisted, however, and the U.S. Commissioner for Exchange at Fortress Monroe, Virginia, the official exchange point, later made an inquiry. The Confederates informed him, "nothing is known by the citizens of the place, except by a report from the enemy that there was a meeting among those men in which some were killed and the others have not been heard of since."

The local Confederate commander reported another theory:

> Young Mr. Farragut*....says that before he left New Orleans, his uncle, Admiral Farragut, said to him that they bombarded this place because they thought these men were killed by the citizens of Pascagoula, but afterwards found out that the men (Feds) had mutinied and killed their officer and others, and the remainder, or mutineers, had never been heard of since.

Was this a genuine mutiny? Was Chase another Captain Bligh? How did the rumor about civilian clothes get started? Considering the tedium and chronic breaches of discipline aboard *Maria*, almost anything could have happened. The fire was ready for ignition; what spark ignited it will never be known.

This gruesome incident provided the last break in *Maria's* rou-

---

* Admiral Farragut was familiar with New Orleans and had cousins in the Confederate service. Apparently there was constant writing between Union and Confederate family members.

tine. Without further noteworthy adventures, she continued the wearisome blockade until the end of the war. She was eventually sold out of the service on 6 September 1866 for $5000. This might seem a financial loss, but *Maria* had more than earned her keep. To borrow Admiral Alfred T. Mahan's language, those storm tossed, poorly manned and unseaworthy vessels, in the long run, broke the back of the Confederacy. *Maria* and her consorts more than paid their way.

While Admiral Farragut deserves all the honors he has received down through the years, in this case he was too ready to jump to the wrong conclusion. Acting Master Chase did not desert to the enemy. He died doing his duty and it appears that he died hard in the process. He may not have been the best commander in the service but he did the best he knew how with the unpromising material allotted to him. The simple truth is that he met his end in the line of duty and no service can ask more than that.

*　　*　　*

The entire matter appears in ORN I, 19, 362 *et seq.* under the title "Loss of a boat's crew from the U. S. schooner *Maria A. Wood,* November 21, 1862." Additional information is from the ship's deck log in the National Archives.

CHAPTER IX

"A Long War *and* a Sickly Season"

Yellow Fever and the East Gulf Blockading Squadron

One of the fortunate by-products of the construction of the Panama Canal at the beginning of the twentieth century was the elimination of Yellow Fever by Major Walter Reed and his associates. We do not read much about epidemics of this disease which occurred during the Civil War; however, along with the monotonous routine, blockaders did face this illness and death. Outbreaks of yellow fever had devastating effects on the navy serving in tropical waters.

Yellow fever is an acute viral disease transmitted to humans, tending to be active during warmer weather and to subside with cold. Its incubation period is three to five days after infection (a mosquito bite); it lasts about a week, and it can be fatal. Since there is no specific treatment, the best remedy is to avoid exposure by eliminating the source of the plague, mosquitoes, a method brilliantly employed in the case of the Panama Canal. Unfortunately that was years in the future; in Civil War times it was supposed the disease was spread by contact between humans and so the deceased victims were often given immediate burial.[1]

In the days of fighting sail, the favorite toast among

junior officers was "A long war or a sickly season," honoring the two principal causes of their promotion: death and pestilence. During the Civil War junior officers in the United States Navy, in particular the East Gulf Blockading Squadron (whose jurisdiction extended from St. Andrew's Bay, east of Pensacola to Cape Canaveral, including the Bahamas and Cuba) benefitted from both at once.

*　　*　　*

Two epidemics of Yellow Fever particularly affected the East Gulf Blockading squadron, the first in 1862 and the second in 1864. On 1 August 1862, Flag Officer James L. Lardner reported to the Navy Department from his flagship *San Jacinto* at Key West:

> It is with the greatest regret that I am obliged to report that the yellow fever has broken out in this ship. There are 9 cases on the surgeon's report today, and 2 have previously died of that disease.... There is no proper hospital for contagious diseases at Key West... Carrying the yellow fever so near our troops at Pensacola is not to be thought of therefore...I have directed Commander Ronckendorf to proceed with the *San Jacinto*...to Boston.

On 30 August 30 1862, Acting Ensign Simeon N. Freeman, the third senior officer of USS *R. R. Cuyler*, similarly reported to the Navy Department:

> On the 21st, our surgeon being very sick and also several of the men, we steered for the N.E. Channel...At 10 p.m. we fell in with the USS *Huntsville* and applied to him for assistance, but he could not render us any as his surgeon had died that morning and he was on his way to Key West for advice, a number of his officers and men lying dangerously ill...On the night of 22nd instant Commander F. Winslow was taken seriously ill with fever. We arrived at Nassau on the 23d...where we obtained medical advice from HMS *Melpomene*...The same day Lieutenant J.V. Philip was taken down with the fever and also several men....The surgeon advised lying off the port until next morning as he considered the captain's

case a very dangerous one....On the 25th a consultation of the officers was held, and came to the conclusion that the shortest and only way to make the ship efficient was to proceed to some Northern port where we could get the sickness out of the ship, appoint new officers to her and put to sea again....On the 25th we steered for New York. On the 26th....Commander Francis Winslow departed this life. His body has been preserved and will be transmitted to his friends...I am happy to report that Lieutenant Philip and Dr. Watson are recovering and that the malignant symptoms that were so prevalent....have already disappeared.

The Surgeon of the Fleet reported on December 24, 1862, that twenty-four vessels of the navy and merchant service had been infected with the fever in Key West harbor within the past five months.

Bad as these conditions were in 1862, it was far worse in 1864. On 19 June of that year Admiral Theodorus Bailey, the squadron commander, ordered USS *Tioga* north, the first of many to be sent from the blockade. On 27 July, Bailey reported to the department:

My worst fears have been more than realized and for more than two months the disease has held its course without abatement and is now as virulent as at any time. The season of epidemic lasted in 1862 nearly till the 1st of November and there seems to be no reason to believe that it will disappear sooner the present year, except it shall have exhausted all the material for disease before that time...The mortality on the island [Key West] I am told has reached as high as 12 to 15 in a day...

On the ordinance ship *Dale*, I believe every person has been taken except Commander Handy and a boatswain's mate...I myself had the disease in a severe form, as did also Mr. Zeller, the fleet engineer, Mr. Bowman, the secretary, Passed Assistant Surgeon Richardson, the quartermaster, all the servants, and indeed every person attached to these headquarters but one...The doctor...was taken the fourth day after his arrival and died the third day after his attack. The *Huntsville* has had from 20 to 30 cases. Her sick list for today shows 14 cases, and those assuming a more malignant type than the previous ones...The other vessels in which the disease has appeared are the *Honduras*, the *Iuka*, the *Marigold*, the *Honeysuckle* and the *San Jacinto* [again]. Deaths have occurred of officers and men on those vessels.

On 7 August, with the permission of the Navy Department, Admiral Bailey himself went north in *San Jacinto*, which, after this second round of infection, must have had a reputation as a plague ship. Command of the squadron was turned over to Captain Theodore P. Greene in Key West. Within a week the new commander was presented with his worst case, that of USS *James S. Chambers*.

Chambers was a 3 masted schooner remarkably similar in dimensions to *Maria A. Wood*. Purchased in 1861, she had been employed as a blockader up and down both coasts of Florida. On 21 July 1864, under the command of Acting Master Luther Nickerson, she anchored off Indian River on the east coast, relieving USS *Roebuck* on the blockade. Here her tragedy commenced.

We now know that the disaster began with the anchoring. Nickerson anchored within mosquito range of the coast; had he moved farther out, or kept moving, he might well have avoided the epidemic, as the fever obviously had not come aboard at Key West when he left eleven days earlier. That the anchorage was to blame is corroborated by the fact that *Roebuck*, her predecessor on that station, arrived at Key West with such a number of fever cases that she eventually had to be sent north.[2]

Extracts from *Chambers'* log and reports paint a grim picture:

Acting Master Nickerson to Admiral Bailey, 5 August 1864:
There has not been anything of importance since my arrival at this station, other than I regret to report an unusual amount of sickness on board. It broke out about ten days ago; it assumed the form of an epidemic. My surgeon was among the first taken; he has not yet recovered, but is improving. Over one-third of my crew are on the list; the sickness is very debilitating, but no cases are fatal as yet.[3]

On the 5th, shortly after Nickerson had dispatched this report, Thomas Hale, seaman, and James McCloskey, landsman, died of fever. On 6 August, "The threatening appearance of the weather and debilitated state of the crew compelled the burial...[of Hale and McClosky] at sea.[4] By 9 August the epidemic was raging and Nickerson reported to Bailey:

> [T]he sickness on this vessel has assumed the form of a most malignant fever and increased to an alarming extent. Today we have on sick and binnacle list 38, over two-thirds of our number. Three of my officers were taken down last night and are very sick. I have lost 4 men by death since the 5th instant, burying 1 this morning....I can raise barely enough well men to man a boat....

From this point on all reports and entries in the log were signed by Acting Ensign William J. Eldredge, the third senior officer on board.

Extract from the log, 10 August:
At 4 a.m. Henry L. Simon, OS [Ordinary Seaman] died of fever. At 4:15 a.m. buried Henry L. Simon at sea. At 6:10 a.m. Jos. Holdsby OS died of fever. At 10:15 buried Jos. Holdsby at sea. At 4:35 p.m. H.C. Chace, Yeoman, died of fever. Sick list 35.[5]

This pattern of hasty burial repeats itself all through the course of the epidemic but even burial at sea became difficult. Eldredge reported to Bailey, that not even a boat's crew could be raised in the crew of the strong and able, burials were made by dropping a cutter with the bodies aboard astern, with the current to a distance of 600 yards, her crew of 3 or 4 men dragging the heavy boat back to the ship by a line fastened for the purpose. Still, the dreadful toil did not abate:

August 11 At 2 a.m. Jos. Stebbins, QM, died of fever. At 7:30 H.S. Chace and Jos. Stebbins buried at sea. At 1:30 p.m. Alex. Watts LDS [landsman] died of fever and was buried at sea. At 8:45 p.m. Hiram Cripps OS died of fever. Sick list 30.

Robert Smalls, pilot of the Confederate gunboat Planter. *Smalls and eight other black crewmen commandeered the ship at Charleston, South Carolina in May, 1862 and sailed out to the Federal fleet. Such "contrabands" aided the Union navy on many occasions, such as the rescue of the* James S. Chambers. *(As reported in* Harper's Weekly, *June 14, 1862.)*

August 12 At 4 a.m. Hiram Cripps buried at sea. At 3:40 p.m. Michael Gleason, Capt. Hold, died of fever. At 4:30 p.m. Michael Gleason buried at sea. At 8:15 p.m. Henry McKenzie GM [Gunner's Mate] in Charge died of fever.

August 13 At 4:45 a.m. Actg. Ensign Henry E. Hopkinson died of fever. At 6:45 a.m. Gunner's Mate McKenzie and Ensign Hopkinson were buried at sea.

Unknown to the distraught Nickerson and Eldredge, help was under way. Captain Greene, who had relieved Admiral Bailey as squadron commander, had, on receipt of Nickerson's August 9 report, forthwith dispatched the steam tug *Honeysuckle* with an additional doctor, medical stores, ice and eight "contrabands"*to

---

* Contrabands were escaped slaves, so called because of the ingenious theory that, their owners being at war with the United States, their property somehow became "contraband of war." Thousands of such escaped slaves rendered useful service to the Union forces during the war.

the aid of the stricken schooner. *Honeysuckle* arrived about noon on the 13th.

> **August 13** Signalized *Honeysuckle* for [her] captain to repair [come] on board. After consulting with him and Passed Surgeon Macomber...together with surgeon attached to this ship, and all deeming it humane and justifiable, being unable to keep the blockade, to get North as soon as possible, at 12:50 got underway and stood to the Northward.

Nickerson's (or Eldredge's—the log does not make it clear) decision to quit his post must not have been an easy one. In 1862 Rear Admiral David G. Farragut had reproved Commander Henry French of *Albatross* for leaving his post because of a yellow fever outbreak, saying, "Our duties in war are imperative, and we are as much bound to face the fever as the enemy," and French had a report from his surgeon to the effect that it was "indispensable to the health and safety of the crew" to do so.[6] No reproof ever came to Eldredge from the Navy Department so it is fair to assume that this was an acceptable decision.

Greene had prepared for *Chambers'* assistance as thoroughly as possible; in the light of Nickerson's reports, clearly *Chambers* could not remain at her station. Nevertheless it must have been a fearful responsibility for an acting officer of a junior grade to take, with or without a council of war.

Once he got off the coast and away from the mosquitoes, Eldredge suffered but two more deaths from fever. The first was that of James Slavin, a seaman. The second, and more painful to Eldredge, is recorded in the log:

> **August 15** At 1:15 a.m. Act. Master Luther Nickerson commanding died of fever. At 8:15 p.m. by advice of Surgeon buried at sea. At 1:15 p.m. Surgeon F. J. Williams was seized of nervous debility and insanity brought on by overexertion, anxiety and attention to the sick for many days previous.

Another tragedy occurred later that same day:

August 15 At 6:15 p.m. Actg. Master's Mate John T. Van Nest in, it is supposed, a fit of derangement jumped overboard and was drowned, in spite of every effort to save him. Lat.35.12 N; Long. 75.10 W.

When Van Nest jumped overboard, he left Eldredge the only officer fit for duty, surely an onerous burden for any junior officer. On August 24 *Chambers* anchored off the Philadelphia Quarantine station and Eldredge forthwith dispatched a final report to Secretary of the Navy Gideon Welles:

> **At Quarantine, near Philadelphia, August 14, 1864**
> As this vessel has been brought by me from her station in the East Gulf Blockading Squadron without orders from the officer in command of said squadron, I beg leave to lay before you the following statement:
> Our captain and executive officer being down sick, the command devolved on myself. There remained but one other officer fit for duty, Acting Master's Mate J.F. Van Nest...

Not long afterward the strain affected the overworked physician:

> **Sept. 11,** 11. Surgeon F. J. Williams while in a state of insanity became furious and was put in a straight jacket.

Chambers remained at anchor in the stream at least until September 13 when her deck log closed abruptly with no mention of either docking or decommissioning. The next entry begins in November 1864 with a new volume and new officers and crew. At the end of the war she was still serving, as were most of her stricken consorts. Some forty years later, far too late for their war, the disease was controlled forever.

*   *   *

The best way to piece together the story of the epidemic is to examine the records in ORN I, 17, as indexed under the heading

"Yellow Fever." *Chambers'* deck log is in the National Archives in Washington. It is unusual in that it is not in the typical deep sea format but in the type of log used for vessels serving in inland waters. The succeeding volume, beginning in November 1864, is in the usual format.

CHAPTER X

The Aftershocks of the *Florida*

The Confederate Navy began the Civil War with the very few ships taken from the North at the outset of the war. With limited repair facilities and lacking ships, the South was forced into the use of irregular activities to carry the naval war to the Union. The foremost of these was the use of commerce raiders, primarily obtained from England.

Because of an English law prohibiting the building and arming of warships for a belligerent power, the South employed stealth and deception to get ships built. One of these methods was to have a ship built ostensibly for a foreign power and arm her either at sea or in the port of a weak neutral power. While the most famous of these commerce raiders was the *Alabama*, she was followed by others, one of which was the *Florida*, originally known as *Oreto*.

From her first days to her last, *Florida* was trouble for the United States Navy. Built in Liverpool ostensibly for the Italian government, she was copied from, and reportedly was a duplicate of, an English warship: 190 feet long, barque rigged with two engines—she was beautiful, efficient and deadly.

Of course, *Florida* was neither the first, the last, nor even the most famous commerce raider of the Civil War. A contemporary to her near-sister *Alabama*, her fame is overshadowed by that well-known vessel. Yet *Florida* played a significant role in the conflict, and it is fair to say she paid her way. During her two and a half year career, she contributed to the mortification of the Union commanders whose job it was to stop her. This is the story of how she affected four of them.

*   *   *

1. The Abrupt Dismissal of Commander Preble

Although the Confederacy would have liked to keep it secret, *Florida's* construction did not go unnoticed by the United States Government. During her building in Liverpool in the winter of 1861-1862, the American ambassador, Charles Francis Adams, twice called the attention of the British Foreign Office to her character as a warship; but he obtained no satisfaction in his attempt to have her construction halted.[1] Sailing unarmed from Liverpool on 22 March 1862 and cleared for Palermo, Sicily, *Florida* diverted to Nassau in the Bahamas where she arrived 28 April. A few days later she was joined by the steamer *Bahama,* which had sailed from England the same day as *Florida* and which carried for her the guns and ammunition which could not legally have been installed in England.

On the complaint of the United States consul in Nassau that the entire transaction was a gross violation of English law, she was impounded custody by the local authorities but, after a delay of several months, was released by a sympathetic court. In company with *Bahama,* she sailed to one of the remote Bahama keys where her two 7 inch rifles and six 6 inch guns were taken on board, and she was duly commissioned as the Confederate cruiser *Florida* under the command of Lieutenant John Newland Maffitt CSN. Her crew was minimal: five firemen and fourteen deck hands.

Captain James N. Maffit, commander of the Florida. *His daring exploits were somewhat overshadowed by the more famous Confederate raider* Alabama.

Maffitt himself had to pitch in and lend a hand transferring the supplies from *Bahama* to *Florida*.

As soon as possible, Maffitt took her to Cuba where almost the entire crew, including Maffitt and his stepson, came down with yellow fever. Maffitt's own case was so bad that a Cuban doctor pronounced him beyond recovery; the stepson died. With his crew so obviously crippled, Maffitt determined to go to Mobile, Alabama, and complete his ship and crew there.

Six steam gunboats and the steam frigate *Susquehanna* customarily made up the Mobile blockading force. Just before Maffitt's arrival, *Susquehanna* had departed for repairs, and three of the gunboats were at Pensacola for repairs or coal. The steam gunboats *Winona, Cayuga,* and *Oneida* under Commander George H. Preble USN composed the remaining force. Preble, the senior officer present and thus in tactical command of the force, was the grandson of Commodore Edward Preble, an early hero of the Tripolitan Wars. He had distinguished himself in command of a gunboat under Flag Officer David G. Farragut and had been given command of *Oneida* as a reward. Preble further reduced his force by ordering *Cayuga* to the westward to examine some unguarded passes, leaving only two blockaders to guard the principal entrance to the bay. The chief engineer of *Oneida* had reported a leak in the port boiler "which was so large as to necessitate the almost constant use of the donkey pump." Preble granted permission to draw the fire of that boiler early in the morning of 4 September, but, although repairs had been completed during the afternoon and fires were started under it, a working pressure had not been obtained at the time *Florida* came in sight about five in the afternoon.

Maffitt's breakthrough was simple and direct. He hoisted the colors displayed by a vessel of the Royal Navy and steamed towards the blockaders, relying upon his resemblance to a British warship. Preble, not knowing that both *Florida* and *Alabama* had left England, assumed that she was, in fact, what she appeared to be. He went to general quarters and laid a course to pass close to *Florida's* port beam. When Preble failed to obtain a reply to his hail, he first fired three shots across *Florida's* bow and when, she still did not reply or stop, he then fired his entire starboard broadside into her. When USS *Winona* and the armed schooner *Rachel Seaman*, which had just arrived, joined in the fire, Maffitt ordered the British colors struck and his Confederate colors raised. While the quartermaster was carrying out this order, he had one of his fingers taken off by shrapnel, and the Confederate colors never were raised.

Florida never slowed down, and Preble continued firing until, in three fathoms of water and with darkness coming on, he abandoned the chase and returned to his station. During his twenty-four minute pursuit, Preble fired thirty-five times at *Florida*, inflicting severe damage; in fact, considerably more than Preble conceived. Maffitt later assessed *Oneida's* impact:

The fire from this vessel, the *Oneida*, increased in warmth and destruction, carrying away all the standing and most of the running rigging of my vessel...During all this time shell and shrapnel were bursting over us and around us, the shrapnel striking the hull and spars at almost every discharge...When we anchored under the guns of Fort Morgan...the *Florida* was a perfect wreck, and only succeeded in escaping by the smoothness of the sea and her superior speed...If there had been any sea on[,] our bilge pumps would not have saved the vessel from sinking...It took three and a half months to repair her.

The rapid pace of events and the twilight hid most of this damage from Preble and his superiors for some time, and both Admiral David G. Farragut and the Navy Department chastised *Oneida* for poor gunnery, the reason supposed by them to have been the reason for the cause of the failure to prevent *Florida*'s rush into port. The department went even further; long before *Florida* was ready for sea, George Preble had ceased to be an officer in the United States Navy.

The same night that *Florida* slipped by the blockade, Preble sent a hastily composed report to his superior, Admiral Farragut, at Pensacola. Woefully lacking in detail, it generated a prompt and severe reaction. On 8 September Farragut forwarded Preble's report to Secretary of the Navy Gideon Welles, introducing it ominously: "I regret to be compelled again to make another mortifying acknowledgement of apparent neglect." He went on, "Why Captain Preble did not fire into her after she failed to stop or answer his hail, I cannot imagine...[T]here never was a finer opportunity for stopping a vessel until she passed them; then, however, when it was too late, they commenced firing."

The Navy Department's reaction can best be described as brutal. Secretary of the Navy Gideon Welles wrote in his diary entry for 9 September:

Preble, by sheer pusillanimous neglect, feebleness and indecision, let the pirate steamer *Oreto* [*Florida*] run the blockade....This case must be investigated and an example made.

The next day Welles continued in his diary:

There must be a stop put to the timid, hesitating and I fear sometimes traitorous conduct of some of our officers....The time has arrived when these derelictions must not go unpunished....Preble is not a traitor, but loyal. An educated gentlemanly officer of a distinguished family and more than ordinary acquirements, but wants promptitude, energy, decision, audacity, perhaps courage....A man less versed in books would have sunk the pirate if she did not stop when challenged.[2]

Consequently Welles issued the following order dated Saturday, 20 September:

Commander George Henry Preble, senior officer in command of the blockading force off Mobile having been guilty of neglect of duty in permitting the armed steamer *Oreto* to run the blockade thereby not only disregarding Article 36, Sec. 10th of the Articles of War which requires an officer to "do his utmost to overtake and capture or destroy every vessel which it is his duty to encounter," but omitting the plainest ordinary duty committed to an officer is, by order of the President, dismissed from the naval service from this date.

The commander of each vessel of war on the day after the receipt of this published order will cause it to be read on the quarter deck at general muster together with the accompanying reports and enter both upon the vessel's log.

The verbatim text of Preble's report and Farragut's endorsement was appended to this order.

On the same day Welles wrote directly to Preble:

SIR: Rear-Admiral Farragut has transmitted to the Department your letter addressed to him on the 4th instant, in which you report that on the afternoon of that day a vessel "carrying four quarter boats and a battery of eight broadside guns, one or two pivots, and having every appearance of an English man-of-war, ran the block-ade," and of her approach you had abundant notice, and when abeam of her, about 100 yards distant, you hailed her, fired repeatedly across her bow, over and at her, but she managed by "superior speed and unparalleled audacity" to enter the harbor of Mobile. Upon submitting your letter to the President, I received from him prompt directions to announce to you your dismissal from the service. You will from this date cease to be regarded an officer of the Navy of the United States.

The idea of dismissing Preble did not originate with President Lincoln. Welles' diary entry for 20 September 1862 records, "I then took the dispatches to the President and submitted them to him. He said promptly: 'Dismiss him. If that is your opinion, it is mine. I will do it.' I am sorry for Preble, but shall be sorry for my country if it is not done."[3]

It is difficult today to justify such an arbitrary procedure, taken in haste and without the remotest semblance of due process of law. Farragut's report did arrive at the Navy Department during the battle of Antietam, one of the most critical of the Civil War and Abraham Lincoln may well have been preoccupied by that event and his forthcoming Emancipation Proclamation. A commander's failure to do his utmost could not have come at a worse time, or Lincoln, himself a good lawyer and an eminently fair man, might possibly have realized the lack of due process and overruled Welles.

While this sequence of documents was working its way up to Washington and back, Preble took *Oneida* to Pensacola. On 6 September he forwarded a second and more complete report. Still he suspected nothing until 8 October, when he read of his fate in a newspaper. He at once protested vehemently to Farragut:

SIR: Unseen and unheard, while engaged in distant service, I learn from the columns of a newspaper that my name has been struck from the rolls of the Navy, after twenty-seven years' honorable servitude...The poorest boy or man in the service has for his petty offenses the privilege of a summary court-martial and a hearing. Through you I respectfully request from the Navy Department a court of inquiry into my conduct on this occasion, and would willingly have it extended through my whole term of service in the Navy...I court a full and complete investigation.

He concluded his plea:

The President recommended me by name for the thanks of Congress in the passage of the Forts [on the Mississippi]...and subsequent capture of New Orleans...He next promotes me to the rank which had justly been my due for six months previous, and now, on insufficient and incomplete evidence, he directs that my name be stricken from the rolls of the Navy, and that a record of my disgrace be placed upon every log book and read to the assembled crews of every ship in commission. This is hard usage, and small consideration for one who today completes his twenty-seventh year of service.[4]

Preble remained in command of *Oneida* until officially receiving his order of dismissal from the Navy Department on 12 October 1862. He was relieved by Lieutenant Commander Montgomery Sicard.[5] *Oneida's* deck log reflects the tension on board during the change in command, recording that on 14 October seven men were logged for one or more of the following offenses: going below on watch; not cleaning priming wire; not behaving properly at quarters and loafing in the wardroom. On 15 October, the day Captain Thornton A. Jenkins assumed command, five individuals were logged for one or more of the following: going below on watch; neglect of duty; not paying attention, and disrespect to an officer. On that day "Capt. Preble with his clerk, Mr. Dalton, left the ship and went to the *Rhode Island*."

Preble had begun his campaign for reinstatement even before he left. On 10 October he addressed a third and more complete report to Farragut as well as a letter to the President demanding "a fair and full and instant investigation...before a court of enquiry." In addition, he sent statements from all his commissioned officers and his gunner and boatswain.

In his reports Preble stressed the resemblance of *Florida* to a

British warship; the necessity of not offending Great Britain[6]; the defective condition of *Oneida*'s boiler which had reduced her speed by several knots and that the previously underestimated damage to *Florida* was more than had been supposed. To further strengthen his case, Preble had addressed a series of questions to each of his subordinate commanders, intended to rebut the hastily drawn dismissal order. In one question he asked them what was their conception of "the plainest ordinary duty committed to an officer," the language used by Welles in his order of 20 September. Predictably (for more than one reason), nobody knew what that duty was.

Preble returned to his home in Massachusetts. There he collected another statement, that of Commander James A. Thornton of the *Winona*. In addition he wrote a book in his defense which he had privately printed, entitled *The Chase of the Rebel Steamer Oreto*. Whether through this book, his efforts, public sentiment, or political pressure, public opinion began to swing in his favor, and officers of the navy and members of Congress began to take his side.

On 10 February 1863 Welles forwarded all documents in the case to President Lincoln with an accompanying letter:

> The Hon. William P. Fessenden, of the Senate, has, on repeated occasions expressed a very earnest desire that the late Commander George Henry Preble should be restored to the naval service. The Naval Committee of the Senate have expressed similar views. Distinguished naval officers and others have also united in his behalf.

After reciting his own version of the facts, Welles concluded grudgingly:

> While I am not prepared to recommend his restoration, I can not, after the request of Senator Fessenden and the Naval Committee, and the appeal that had been made in his behalf by other friends, including the admiral under whom he served...do otherwise than respectfully submit the case...for your consideration.

On 12 February Lincoln nominated Preble to be a commander, retroactive to 16 July 1862. Since this was where he ranked prior to the *Florida* affair, this meant Preble was reinstated without any loss of seniority. He did not succeed in getting the log entries, which had been ordered by Welles to be placed in every deck log in the navy, expunged.

Preble never got back in Welles' good graces. He was demoted from the steam warships he had commanded to the sail sloop *St. Louis*, then in European waters. He remained in command of her for the rest of the war. During this exile, he had one final glimpse of *Florida*. On 12 March 1864 he reported to Welles from Funchal, Madeira:

> The *Florida* has succeeded in getting to sea. I shall follow her at once, though hopeless of catching her out of port. Nelson said the want of frigates in his squadron would be found impressed on his heart. I am sure the want of steam will be found engraven on mine. Had the *St. Louis* been a steamer, I would have anchored alongside of her, and unrestricted by the twenty-four hour rule, my old foe could not have escaped me.[7]

Preble's later career was respectable if not distinguished. He was promoted to captain in 1867, commodore in 1871, and rear admiral in 1876. He retired in 1878 and died in 1885.[8] The *Florida* affair had still galled him however, and when he obtained sufficient rank to be able to do something about it, he did just that.

On 20 April 1872 a court of inquiry was convened "to investigate the circumstances attending the entrance" of the *Florida* into Mobile Bay. This tribunal heard Preble and his friend Thornton, two of the Federal commanders present on the scene. Preble then called John Newland Maffitt, his former adversary,* to the stand.

Maffitt confirmed the effect of *Oneida*'s fire and the decimation of his crew. He testified that he had sent all his crew below decks

---

* It would be more than seventy-three years before the Navy would again see the commander of an enemy warship testify respecting the conduct of one of its own commanding officers. On 13 December 1945 Commander Mochitsura Hashimoto IJN testified at the court martial of Captain Charles B. McVay III, charged after the sinking of USS *Indianapolis* on 30 July, 1945.

except himself and two men at the helm and described graphically the damage wrought by *Oneida*'s fire. He pointed out that "one XI shell" struck the forward boiler, decapitating one man and wounding nine others. The total casualties were one dead and ten wounded out of a crew of twenty-two, or fifty per cent. Maffitt's testimony certainly disproved the charge that Preble had refrained from aggressive action.[9]

The court issued a formal opinion that, after restating the facts in language favorable to Preble, concluded with the finding that "the court are of the opinion that [Preble's] failure to take any measures to heave the *Oreto* to...was...a venial violation of duty and that when it became manifest to him that the *Oreto* intended to violate the blockade, he did all that a loyal, brave, and efficient officer could do to capture or destroy her." This lukewarm verdict was as close to vindication as Preble would ever get, and even this would be forgotten when later historians recounted the story of the *Florida*. Admiral David D. Porter characterized Preble as "a prudent, careful officer who tried hard not to commit any mistakes; but on this occasion he was too careful not to compromise his government by attacking the English man-of-war, as he supposed the *Florida* was...[and was] caught napping...He hesitated, however, and his hesitation lost him a prize and the honor of capturing one of the Confederate scourges of the ocean."[10]

Porter's appraisal sums up Preble well, but the inequity of Preble's punishment is clear, and his reassignment to *St. Louis* is unfortunate. Had he been left in command of *Oneida* at Mobile, he would have been the person least likely to be caught napping twice, and it is a pity that he never got the chance to prove it.

2. The Dismay of Commodore Hitchcock

Commodore Robert T. Hitchcock had been in Pensacola for repairs to his flagship *Susquehanna* when *Florida* ran past Federal blockaders and entered Mobile Bay, and so escaped the censure which fell on Preble. Now back on the blockade, Hitchcock knew he had to keep *Florida* bottled up in Mobile Bay, for he had George Preble's fate as an example.

*   *   *

On paper Commodore Hitchcock's task seemed simple. Mobile Bay, some thirty miles in length and from ten to twenty miles in width, is the outlet for the Alabama and Tombigbee Rivers and contains the port of Mobile, through which a large portion of the maritime commerce of the South flows. The Federals had blockaded this valuable port from the beginning of the war; it was now Hitchcock's task to keep *Florida* blockaded.

Despite its size, the bay compresses into a five mile wide opening between Fort Morgan to the east and Fort Gaines on the west. While at that time two side or "swash" channels existed and were used by lighter draft vessels, the only practical route for vessels of *Florida's* size was a comparatively straight channel, running some five miles to seaward from a point directly under the guns of Fort Morgan, almost astride the channel. This ante-bellum brick and stone structure so controlled the channel that eventually the combined efforts of an entire fleet were needed to defeat it. From the viewpoint of a blockader, they were safe providing they kept at a respectful distance.

Abutting the west side of the channel, nearly three miles to seaward of Fort Morgan, was half-mile-long Sand Island, where a conspicuous, abandoned lighthouse provided perfect cover for a blockader to lurk behind, unobtrusive and hard to discern. Mobile Bay thus resembled a gigantic water bottle whose contents must necessarily pour through a narrow spout. The other exits were, with the exception of the swash channels, either too shallow for *Florida* or not navigable at all. Single pickets could cover each of the swash channels, giving the advantage to the blockaders. An escaping vessel had to go nearly five miles straight down a restricted channel before it could safely take evasive action. Hitchcock stationed the blockading vessels in a position akin to a strainer ready to arrest any object poured through the spout.

At all times Hitchcock had at his disposal a minimum of seven vessels in addition to his own command, *Susquehanna*. While this force included a collection of hastily built or acquired vessels, it also included two ships considered to be equal or superior to *Florida*: *Oneida*, Preble's old command, and *R.R. Cuyler*, one of the fastest ships in the Navy. Hitchcock assigned two gunboats to each swash channel. In the main channel he stationed another gunboat, *Pembina*, as a picket going inside the bar whenever it was safe, supported by his own ship, *Susquehanna*. With *R.R. Cuyler* just on the east side of the channel abreast of *Pembina*, and *Oneida* just on the west side abreast of his flagship, Hitchcock believed that this arrangement would serve to contain the Confederates. However, he underestimated his adversary, John Newland Maffitt.

Maffitt needed all the time he could get to make preparations for sea, since his vessel had been heavily damaged on the run in and it was not until January 1863 that he was ready to make his move. While waiting, he could bask in fame but little else. The secretary of the Confederate Navy, Stephen Mallory, had declined to promote him for his spectacular run into the bay on the rather flimsy theory that, since *Florida*'s guns had not actually been mounted, the service was civil rather than military.[11]

Maffitt's journal* does not disclose when *Florida* dropped down

---

* Maffitt kept a journal very similar to the entries in a ship's log, making a rough draft and thereafter refining it into a smooth journal. The latter together with the log of *Florida* was later thrown into the sea by him while running the blockade into Charleston. A rough journal, however, survived and extracts from it appear in ORN I, 2, 667 et seq.

from Mobile to Fort Morgan, but she was certainly there by 13 January because on that date he took *Florida* down to the bar and back. On the 14th, in miserable weather, he tried again to get out but abandoned an "ineffectual effort" to escape. Notwithstanding these two previous ventures, it was not until the 15th that a lookout on *Oneida* identified the blockade runner "laying under Fort Morgan." Despite the heavy weather which had persisted for the past three days, Hitchcock ordered his ships closer to the channel by half the usual distance. In addition, he sent *Pembina* around to the other vessels with orders for *Cuyler* and *Oneida* to act as chasers in the event of an escape. As a final precaution he made the general signal "*Oreto* expected out; keep full steam.*"

Despite these warnings, and the conspicuous humiliation of his ship by *Florida* when she ran into Mobile, Captain Samuel Hazard of *Oneida* was not on the alert. At 4:45 in the afternoon he recorded that he "came to anchor in 10 fathoms water, veered to 75 fathoms chain prepared to slip." From that time on nothing but normal routine is recorded in his log.

Accounts of Maffitt's escape differ in all but one area; the two adversaries agreed that the weather was bad. The Federals recorded high winds and heavy seas, while Maffitt concedes it was blowing "with avidity," although he also records that, although earlier it had been too dark to see Lighthouse [Sand] Island, at 2 a.m., the stars were out with a light mist on the surface. *Florida*, Maffitt went on to say, "At 2:40 passed a gunboat anchored just inside the bar, then a second one, but when abreast of the third a flame from the coal dust caused our discovery, and the ocean was lit up by the lights from the nine blockading vessels." However, no mention of flames from *Florida's* stacks appears in any Federal account.

Susquehanna recorded that at 3:15 *Pembina* made a signal

---

* Oreto was the name of Maffit's vessel before he commissioned her as Florida and Union officers frequently referred to her by that name.

"Vessel running out of this pass." *Oneida's* log blandly reports that "At 3:25 *Susquehanna* burnt white and red light, we went to quarters....At 3:50, we having seen no vessel running out beat a retreat." Only *R.R. Cuyler* acted with dispatch, signalling "steamer running out" at 3:30 and commencing a chase which was to last nearly three months.

Maffitt's comments on his escape are charitable, to say the least:

> Our passing unseen by the first Federal gunboats is hard to account for. My idea is that during the severity of the storm, and with them expecting us, a very anxious lookout had been kept, and that when the weather moderated all were exhausted and...concluded that if we had not already escaped no attempt would be made that morning. I believe that had it not been for our soft coal, we would have passed clear.

Hitchcock's patience surely gave out when, at four a.m., the rising moon revealed to him his other chase vessel, *Oneida*, riding serenely at anchor instead of in pursuit of *Florida*, by then long gone.*

If Hazard in *Oneida* was asleep when *Florida* went past him, Commander George F. Emmons in *R.R. Cuyler* was not. Taking the deck partly dressed upon the sighting of *Florida*, he had a signal made to *Susquehanna*, ordered the cable slipped, the crew called to quarters and had *Cuyler* turning in pursuit of her prey, all within four minutes. Accompanied by *Pembina* which, on her commander's own initiative, chased with vigor for some twelve hours, he took off in pursuit of the escaping raider.

> Under all steam and sail that I could raise, I continued the chase all day in a combing sea that kept the decks covered with water and the propeller racing part of the time... [P]ropeller got unhooked on a sea and was stopped for a few minutes, when it was lashed and

---

* She did not commence her chase until the afternoon of the 17th, and when she did it was nearly a month before she was returned to him.

not stopped again until we arrived off the western end of Cuba. Resorted to every effort to increase the speed of the vessel, which varied from $11\frac{1}{2}$ to $12\frac{1}{2}$.

He added with wry humor: "From fancying myself near promotion in the morning, I gradually dwindled down to a court of inquiry at dark, when I lost sight of the enemy."[12]

In *Pembina* under the command of Lieutenant Commander William G. Temple, the chase was also tense:

> The wind was W.S.W., so that the square sail would not stand, and indeed it was too strong a gale to set either this or the fore-gaff topsail... The sea was so heavy that the propeller was constantly thrown entirely out of the water, and raced to an alarming degree;...the engineer...having been ordered to run as fast as he dared with anything like safety to the engine. By half past 5 [p.m.], however, the *Cuyler* had drawn ahead so far that we had lost sight of her and her light.

The chase was closer than either Emmons or Temple realized for, at five in the afternoon, *Florida* had sprung her maintopsail yard and was forced to slow down, at which time *Cuyler* pulled to within 3 miles. Since Emmons does not mention this, it is probable that the coming of night and the heavy weather obscured his target. Nevertheless, Maffitt must have wondered during the long chase just how long his luck would hold out, for he later related that the only two Union vessels he ever feared were *Oneida* and *Cuyler*.

Daylight of the 17th found *Florida* alone at sea. Two days later, Maffitt captured the first of *Florida's* many prizes. She entered Havana harbor in the evening, was supplied with coal by the Spanish authorities, and left on the 22nd, capturing another brace of prizes on the way out.

Hitchcock, with memory of Preble's fate vivid in his mind, took immediate steps to clear his own yardarm by doing what Preble had neglected to do until it was too late. He directed inquiries to all his captains asking for the facts as known to them; their opinion of his arrangement of forces off Mobile and, in what way defective;

and, if he had failed in his duty, in what way. As might be expected, all reported favorably except Lieutenant Commander Samuel R. Franklin of *Aroostook* who, while not having been present at the scene, commented that a vessel should have been placed inside the bar (although he added that had he, himself, been in command he would not have done so!). Nevertheless, when ordered to be tried, Hitchcock realistically commented, "I do not expect to get out of the scrape any better than Preble."[13]

Hitchcock escaped the official fury that fell on Preble. Secretary of the Navy Gideon Welles who, in his diary, had revealed an aversion to Preble and dismissed him from the navy without the formality of a trial, writing of *Florida's* escape, merely commented, "Word comes that the *Oreto* [*Florida*] has escaped from Mobile and destroyed some vessels. Our information is vague and indefinite, but I doubt not that it is in the main true." Welles did order a court of inquiry on Hitchcock, but he was never officially condemned.

Hitchcock remained in command of *Susquehanna* and of the blockade until 12 May 1863. He was commandant of the Norfolk Navy Yard when he was placed on the retired list in 1866. He never became a rear admiral, a rank which was eventually attained by Preble. Admiral Farragut, in his report to the Navy Department, does not condemn Hitchcock but places the blame squarely on Hazard's failure to make effective use of *Oneida*. Hazard was ordered to undergo a court of inquiry but here, again, the records are silent as to what actually occurred. Hazard's report[14] of his actions vacillated and failed to convince Hitchcock and Farragut that he was not to blame for the escape of *Florida*. While on the chase of *Florida*, his health was found to be so bad that a medical survey condemned him as unfit for duty. He was relieved of his command and shipped North where he retired 11 November 1863 and died in 1867.[15]

Writing years after the war, Admiral David D. Porter, who had no direct knowledge of the event, states that *Florida* passed directly between *Cuyler* and *Susquehanna* at a distance of 300 yards from the former and adds "it is stated that half an hour was lost in the

Cuyler's getting away, owing to a regulation of the ship that the officer of the watch should report to the captain and wait for him to come on deck before slipping the cable."[16] In fact, *Cuyler* appears to have been the only vessel to respond correctly.

It does seem that the blame assigned to Hazard was merited; Hitchcock's dispositions seem the most efficient use of the forces available to him. The only defense for Hazard is that he had been in command only two days. In a ship which had just been so disgraced by her adversary, however, the sight of her enemy should have excited her crew rather than put them to sleep. In any event, *Florida* got out, to the serious detriment of the North. Rear Admiral David D. Porter, writing years after the war, wrote: "Every officer who knew Maffitt was certain that he would attempt to get out of Mobile, and we are forced to say that those who permitted his escape are responsible for the terrible consequences of their want of vigilance and energy."

Maffitt continued in command of *Florida* until 18 August 1863 when he entered Brest, France, for supplies and necessary repairs. Shortly after his arrival he came down with heart trouble, possibly a result of the yellow fever he had suffered while in Cuba, and relinquished his command of *Florida*. During his cruise, he took fifty-five prizes, second only to *Alabama* and *Shenandoah*. By comparison, the German *Graf Spee* became famous when she sank nine ships in a later, more modern, war, in which her commander had the advantages of radio and air reconnaissance.

Maffitt's service in warships was thus effectively ended, except for a brief spell in command of the ram *Albemarle* during the summer of 1864. He was relieved of this duty and ordered to sea in command of a blockade runner on 9 September 1864, some six weeks before the spectacular destruction of *Albemarle* on 27 October 1864. (Had Maffitt been in command of *Albemarle* on that date perhaps his ability and ingenuity might very well have saved that ship.) Maffitt returned to the command of blockade runners for the rest of the war. Afterwards, with some diffidence he returned to this country where he died in 1886 in Wilmington,

*Raphael Semmes, captain of the CSS Ala-*bama. *Seen as a romantic figure by pro-Confederate Europeans, he was unsuccessfully tried for treason and piracy by the Federal government.*

N.C. He had been recommended for a position in the Custom House in Wilmington, N.C., but President Grover Cleveland refused to make the appointment, and the news was such a shock to Maffitt that his ailing heart gave out and he died.

In retrospect, he appears actually to have been the dashing raider that Raphael Semmes, the commander of the more celebrated *Alabama*, is generally supposed to have been. Admiral David D. Porter said of Semmes, whom he despised, "[T]he Federal officers captured 1,156 blockade runners during the war. This faithful work was attributed [by Semmes] to the greed of the Old Navy....This, he [Semmes] said, was "the mess of potage" for which so many unprincipled Southern men in the Federal Navy sold their birthright. "Is it any wonder that these loyal men refused to recognize Semmes when he was left by the war in indigent circumstances and could not make a living in the law?"[17] Porter went out of his way, however, to praise Maffitt:

> This officer, it is true, had gone from under the flag we venerate to fight against it; but we know that it was a sore trial for him to leave the service to which he was attached, and that he believed he was doing his duty in following the fortunes of his State, and had the courage to follow his own convictions. He did not leave the United States Navy with any bitterness, and when the troubles were all over he accepted the situation gracefully... [H]e was capable of the greatest heroism and...though he was on the side of the enemy, his courage and skill were worthy of praise.[18]

Maffitt's integrity had been demonstrated when, in January 1861, he was in command of USS *Crusader* off the navy yard at Pensacola, Florida. Maffitt refused to aid the Southern activists then attacking the navy yard and performed his duty to the United States faithfully until he was duly relieved of command. He then resigned his commission and entered the Confederate Navy.

Nevertheless, while the United States Navy has named two destroyers after Semmes, lamentably, no United States naval vessel has ever borne Maffitt's name, a sad repayment for the loyalty he displayed off Pensacola and his unblemished record in command of *Florida*.

3. The Self Destruction of Admiral Wilkes

Florida came into direct contact with the unfortunate Preble and Hitchcock and her effect on their careers was immediate. *Florida* never even came into contact with her next victim, Commodore Charles Wilkes, but because of her, Wilkes, his own worst enemy, destroyed his own career.

*   *   *

Commodore Charles Wilkes was an interesting combination of great ability and equally great instability. One of the older officers on active duty when the war broke out, he had earlier achieved fame as the leader of an expedition to the Antarctic. Through his own intemperate actions, he managed to terminate his career in disfavor and suspension.

Wilkes had achieved general popularity shortly after the inception of the war when, in command of *San Jacinto*, he had intercepted the British mail steamer *Trent* and removed from her two Confederate envoys on their passage to Britain. The United States had only avoided war with that country, outraged by this violation of its neutrality, by a prompt disavowal of Wilkes' act and a return of the envoys; but the general public perceived him as a hero who had once more tweaked the lion's tail. Such adulation would unbalance the judgment of most people and Wilkes already had a mercurial temperament. That he had the President of the United States and the Secretary of State lobbying for him only magnified his ego, and from then on he became a thorn in the flesh of Secretary of the Navy Gideon Welles.

Under pressure from Lincoln and Seward, Welles had offered Wilkes the command of a flotilla to be formed on the James River as a part of the North Atlantic Squadron under Flag Officer Louis M. Goldsborough. Wilkes, like a spoiled child, declined the appointment because it required him to report to Goldsborough. When the command was made independent of Goldsborough, the latter tendered *his* resignation which, though welcomed by Welles for other reasons, did not promote harmony in the department.

Welles had Wilkes' measure to perfection:

> He is very exacting towards others, but is not himself as obedient as he should be. Interposes his own authority to interrupt the execution of orders of the Department... He has abilities but not good judgment in all respects. Will be likely to rashly assume

authority and do things that may involve himself and the country in difficulty.[19]

Nevertheless since the successes of *Florida* and *Alabama* required decisive action at the suggestion of Seward and Lincoln, Wilkes was put in command of a "flying squadron."[20] The newly appointed acting rear admiral justified Welles' fears and turned the command system upside down to the annoyance of the British, the vexation of the Mexicans, the chagrin of the Danish, the gratification of the Confederates, and the exasperation of Welles. The situation came to a head after the escape of *Florida* from Mobile Bay.

Wilkes' "flying squadron" was organized on 8 September 1862, assigning seven vessels and designated "the Western Indies and Bahamas," as its operating area in the search for both *Florida* and *Alabama*. The squadron was given permission to leave the area if in pursuit.[21] Wilkes forthwith assumed command, designating as his flagship the gunboat *Wachusett*.

On 11 January 1863 *Alabama* appeared unheralded before Galveston, Texas, lured the gunboat *Hatteras* from the blockading fleet and sank her in a swift and unequal action, disappearing once more into the mist. Six days later *Florida* made her escape from Mobile Bay, and, after eluding her pursuers *R.R.Cuyler* and *Pembina*, likewise vanished. Discomforting as these events were to Admiral Farragut who commanded in the Gulf, and to Welles, they triggered in Wilkes a frenzy of activity which eventually led to his downfall.

After *Florida*'s escape from Mobile Bay, Welles had decided to intensify the hunt for her by assigning additional vessels outside Wilkes' command to search for and destroy her and her fellow raider Alabama. One of these was the steamer *Vanderbilt*. This vessel was unique even in an expanding navy of unique vessels. Presented to the navy as a gift by Cornelius Vanderbilt in the summer of 1861, some 340 feet in length and rated at a top speed of fourteen knots, she was described by Assistant Secretary of the

Navy Fox as "the only vessel belonging to the United States Navy that will go under steam alone 200 miles a day for 50 days."[22] For her Welles had devised a special mission. On 27 January he ordered *Vanderbilt* to search for *Alabama*, directing her commander, Acting Lieutenant Charles H. Baldwin, to first visit Havana, then "any of the islands, the West Indies or any part of the Gulf.... When you are perfectly satisfied that the *Alabama* has left....and gone to some other locality, you will proceed along the coast of Brazil.... making inquiries at such places as you may think advisable....If at any time word is obtained of the *Alabama*, or any other rebel craft, you will pursue her without regard to these instructions."[23] Baldwin dutifully left the mainland in compliance with these orders.

In the meantime, *Florida* had escaped from Mobile, eluded her pursuers, *Oneida* and *R.R. Cuyler*, and reached Havana. She left that port shortly before the arrival of Wilkes in his flagship, *Wachusett*. Wilkes, on finding *Oneida* there, peremptorily annexed her to his command. Even had he been in good health, her commander, Captain Samuel F. Hazard, was not in a position to protest because of Wilkes' rank. Wilkes' annexation of *Oneida* was so complete that he felt empowered to relieve Hazard, replacing him with *Oneida*'s first lieutenant. Shortly thereafter, falling in with *R.R. Cuyler*, Wilkes likewise annexed her to his command, and then ordered her and *Wachusett* on a ten or twelve day cruise around Cuba. The final straw came in the last week in February when Wilkes fell in with *Vanderbilt*. He liked her so much that he annexed her to his command and made her his flagship.

Given the urgency of finding *Florida*, the geography of the area of action and the communications of the day, a tactful commander just might have been able to pull off these high-handed actions by explaining here, justifying there, and, in general, demonstrating willingness to cooperate with all levels of command. But Wilkes possessed neither wisdom nor tact, and he promptly and with impartial zeal, exasperated all those with whom he dealt. His brusque treatment of those who opposed him illustrates the narrowness of his vision.

To the Governor of Bermuda, who had complained that one of his vessels had anchored in and blocked the fairway [channel], he replied, "I must confess my ignorance of what is meant by the term 'fairway'....In carefully perusing your dispatch...I cannot avoid being struck with some of its peculiar expressions; one of them, 'I have to instruct you that this vessel...can not be permitted to return to these waters.' This I cannot permit; my Government has alone the power of instructing me....It would therefore appear that the remarks in your dispatch...are entirely uncalled for."[24]

He complained to the Governor of Barbados about the permission given *Florida* to coal there: "Your Excellency's excuse...I scarcely believe will be deemed satisfactory to yours or to my Government."[25] He further neglected to inform Admiral Farragut of his annexation of *Cuyler* and *Oneida*, finally brushing it off, some seven weeks after the annexation, with these remarks: "I perhaps owe you an apology for not writing to you a line before...respecting the circumstances in which they fell under my command in the hot pursuit of the *Oreto* [*Florida*] and *Alabama*. I make no doubt [there was] sufficient [reason] to excuse me if any was necessary...I need not, my dear sir, enter into further details, as I well know and believe your views and wishes all correspond with mine."[26]

Wilkes bluntly criticized the Navy Department: "It seems to me somewhat remarkable that you should, under the circumstances, expect captures to be made...The plan at present is, in my judgment, entirely wrong; but in this many differ with me."[27]

His arrogance is again evident in another missive to the Navy Department respecting his conduct towards the British authorities in Nassau: "I would not permit the boats sent out to board me, one from the H.B.M.S. *Barracouta* and another from the governor, whose intention I well knew was to order me [or] desire me to ask permission to anchor, which the pilot told me he had orders to say could not be done. I directed my executive officer to tell the pilot I should anchor when and where I saw fit, and did not intend to ask permission from anybody."[28]

The steamer presented to the Federal government by Cornelius Vanderbilt in 1861, and subsequently named after the donor.

To top it off, Wilkes was a chronic complainer, filling the records with real or pretended grievances, particularly with respect to the ships supplied him, grumbling, "with an inefficient force, both as to numbers and description of vessels...it is utterly impossible for you or the country to expect that it can be accomplished."[29]

This inability to work with others, along with his high-handed acquisition of *Cuyler*, *Oneida* and *Vanderbilt*, led to Wilkes' eventual downfall. On 6 March 1863 Welles directed Wilkes: "Order the *Oneida* and the *R R. Cuyler* to return immediately to Rear-Admiral Farragut, or you may retain the *Cuyler* and send one of your double-end vessels instead."[30]

Wilkes' failure to comply with this order led Welles to again

133

query him on 8 May: "Please inform the Department why the *Oneida* has not been returned to Rear-Admiral Farragut's squadron, agreeably to its order."[31] On 16 June 1863, in reply to this query Wilkes replied, "In my letter of the 2nd of April, I wrote that I intended to return the *Oneida* as soon as she had performed the important service she was then on."[32] This letter added to Welles' determination, made as early as 13 May, to get rid of him. Farragut's understandable anger finally culminated in his complaint to the Navy Department. "It is said that Acting Rear-Admiral Wilkes ignores all authority, and says he will seize all vessels suitable to his purpose until he makes up his number...Should Admiral Wilkes come within my district I shall be strongly tempted to try the working of his system upon himself."[33]

Wilkes commandeered *Vanderbilt* on the theory that his mission superseded that assigned to her by the Navy Department. One can imagine the exasperation of Lieutenant Baldwin, her commander, under strict orders from Welles himself, in being thwarted by Wilkes; not to mention the indignity of having his vessel made Wilkes' flagship, presumably displacing him from the best quarters on board. Since communications would necessarily have to go through Wilkes, Baldwin's ability to complain or advise higher authority of his predicament was blocked.

Baldwin solved the latter problem when on 30 March 1863 he called at Key West and directed a letter to Welles, tactfully pointing out, "I had last the honor of addressing the Department on the 7th instant from Barbados, duplicates of which I enclose. Since that date Rear-Admiral Wilkes has had his flag on board this ship and has no doubt kept the Department informed of her movements. Until the Admiral will permit, I can not, of course, carry out the orders I am under from the Department..."[34] Notwithstanding this report Wilkes did not release *Vanderbilt* until 12 June. As one writer puts it, "The conjunction made it a flat question of whether Wilkes or Welles was running the Navy Department."[35] The result was inevitable; Wilkes was peremptorily ordered to strike his flag and return to Washington. It so happened that Welles' predictions of the course of the Confederate raiders were more accurate than Wilkes'.

While the commandeering of *Oneida* and *Cuyler* may have furnished the justification for Wilkes' relief, the affair of the *Vanderbilt* caused his court martial. Welles manifested his exasperation by relieving Wilkes and placing him on the Retired List. Welles publicly blamed him for the Union navy's failure to check the Confederate raiders, and in his annual report for the year 1863 he stated:

> In derogation of these special and explicit orders [to *Vanderbilt*], Acting Rear Admiral Wilkes on falling in with the *Vanderbilt* transferred his flag to that vessel, and attaching her to his squadron, detained her in his possession so long as to defeat the object and purpose of the department.... The unfortunate detention of the *Vanderbilt* wholly defeated the plans of the department.[36]

Wilkes reacted to this report like a bull to a red rag. On 11 December 1863 he sent Welles a letter which came dangerously close to insolence. The tone of the letter, rather than that of a subordinate to his superior, smacks of a father lecturing an unruly child:

> Upon my return in July last I reported immediately to you, as ordered and requested to know why I was relieved. You replied, "Policy"... This induced me to call upon the Secretary of State, who assured me that my whole course of conduct had met with the approval of the State Department.... It was therefore not my detention of the *Vanderbilt* but your own orders that were carried out.... I am well satisfied that had you looked into the merits of the case you would have awarded credit to me instead of impugning my character as an officer.[37]

This pompous and insubordinate document concluded with the request that it, together with all pertinent correspondence, "may be laid before Congress for my full justification."

In a final, unbelievable, act of folly, Wilkes engineered the delivery of this letter so that copies of it were handed to reporters for the *New York Times* and two other newspapers either before or on the same day that Welles received it. Thus Wilkes not only laid his chest bare for the execution, he delivered the sword to his executioner. In so doing he not only greatly overrated his popularity; he once more greatly underrated Gideon Welles.

First, the infuriated secretary answered him in a letter whose acid tone equalled Wilkes' own, concluding, "The request that your letter...may be laid before Congress for your justification...I shall not comply with, not only because the request is unusual and improper, but because there is no such issue...[Y]ou defeated the plan of the Department, and must not think to escape the consequences of your conduct by any pretext or claim that you would have succeeded in another matter had you not been disappointed."[38]

Welles sent this reply before the story broke in the press on December 18. When it did break, it obviously caused a stir and on 8 January 1864, Welles ordered a Court of Inquiry respecting the publication of Wilkes' letter. Wilkes declined to testify or make a statement, and the Court concluded that he had caused the letter in question to be delivered to the press *before* it was delivered to Welles. Welles then ordered Wilkes to stand trial before a general court martial.

Welles threw every possible charge at Wilkes, including his retention of *Vanderbilt*, *Oneida* and *Cuyler*, the allegedly improper use of *Vanderbilt* in an episode in Venezuela, insubordination in the tone of his letter to Welles of December 11, 1863, the publication of that letter to the press, and Wilkes' failure to properly state his age in a report required of all officers of his rank. Members of the court included four rear admirals (including Goldsborough), four commodores, and Captain John L. Worden of *Monitor* fame. Wilkes promptly challenged Goldsborough, alleging bias because of their earlier dispute and he would appear to have been right. However, although Goldsborough offered to step down, the court declined to permit it.

The record of the trial[39] is of interest only insofar as it reveals Wilkes' mentality. No common law pettifogger ever delved more

Commodore Charles Wilkes, Antarctic explorer and Union naval officer. He has been seen as the U.S. Navy's scapegoat for the exploits of the CSS Florida.

deeply into the realm of technical legal minutiae than did he. Wilkes' arguments contained more ingenuity than merit, and probably served to embroil him deeper in the opinions of his judges. His reasoning would be summarily dismissed by any modern court, but his judges were kinder than any present day tribunal would be, for they listened to him for over a month before arriving at the inevitable conviction.

Wilkes was sentenced to a public reprimand and suspension from duty for three years; he never served again. President Lincoln later modified his sentence and Wilkes became a rear admiral on the Retired List 6 August 1866. He died 8 February 1877, no doubt a bitter and frustrated man.

As the result of this case the regulations concerning the relationship of an independent commander to an area commander of higher rank were modified to provide that in such a case the junior must not be delayed in the execution of his orders "*without an overruling necessity therefor*" (emphasis in the original).[40] However, in Wilkes' case, given his temperament, it is likely that he would have considered the detention of *Vanderbilt* as one of "overruling necessity" and kept her anyway.

It has been said of Wilkes that he had nearly all the qualities of a great admiral and that given a little luck in the West Indies he might have achieved admission to "that small group of men whom posterity has dubbed 'great admirals.'" This is a kinder summation than he deserves, for, spoiled child that he was, he brought his problems on himself. Recently the United States Postal Service issued a stamp commemorating Wilkes. It honors him as "Lt. Charles Wilkes," the rank which he held during his exploration of the Antarctic, the pinnacle of his career and not the rank which he held when he came close to ruining it.

4. The Court Martial of Napoleon Collins

After Maffitt's illness forced him to give up *Florida's* command, she was given to Lieutenant Charles Manigoult Morris CSN. On October 1864 both her famed career and his ended in an incident that strained relations between the United States and friendly Brazil and cast a shadow on the career of Commander Napoleon Collins USN[41]

*　　　*　　　*

Collins, in command of the steam sloop *Wachusett*, had been cruising the South Atlantic looking for *Florida*. He was in the harbor of Bahia, Brazil, on 6 October 1864, when a "strange steamer" came into the port. Someone aboard *Wachusett* must have recognized her for her log records: "At 8:15 [p.m.], the steamer before being anchored in the mouth of the harbor & her movements being suspicious, sent a boat in charge of Mr. Barclay to see what she was. At 8:30 he returned & reported that on hailing the steamer, the answer was that she was the Confederate States steamer *Florida*. Collins promptly "Got up steam, hove short, hoisted in [the] 2nd launch & cleared for action."

Repairs were being made on *Wachusett's* engine, the cylinder heads being off,[42] and she was in the act of replacing her bowsprit. To mislead the Confederates Collins assumed an air of ordinary routine: "Sent market boat as usual." Aboard *Florida* Morris felt sufficiently comfortable in a neutral port to allow his steam to go down, and draw the shot from his guns. He then permitted one watch to go on liberty and went ashore himself with several of his officers.

Morris, who had served in the old navy, should have known better. Scarcely fifty years earlier HMSs *Phoebe* and *Cherub* had battered USS *Essex* to a bloody surrender well inside neutral Chilean waters. Many still living, some yet serving, remembered this well known incident. Indeed, the navy's senior serving officer, Rear Admiral David Glasgow Farragut, had been present at and participated in the action as a midshipman. Morris, knowing the Union's desperate wish to capture *Florida*, certainly should have been aware of it. Nor could he plead ignorance of *Wachusett's* identity. At 7:30 on the evening of the 6th, a boat came alongside stating she was from *Wachusett* with a letter from the U.S. consul addressed to "Captain Morris, sloop *Florida."* [43] The letter was rejected since it was not addressed to "CSS *Florida*." Etiquette aside, no clearer identification of an enemy could possibly be made. Morris, however, entirely missed the point. He therefore missed the opportunity to sell *Florida* to *Wachusett* as dearly as Raphael Semmes had sold *Alabama* to USS *Kearsarge* a few months earlier;[44] and he missed his own place in history.

If *Florida* was not prepared, *Wachusett* was. During the afternoon, a delegation from the lower deck approached Collins saying that they "were with him to the last man in whatever action he took—diplomacy or no diplomacy," and further hinting that they would rather be expatriates in Brazil than return to the United

States and face the rest of the fleet after the news of their chance to take *Florida* came out. Emboldened, no doubt, by this show of support, Collins held a council of war in his cabin to perfect the details of the attack. Among other things he ordered that all attackers tie a white cloth around their left arms for identification. Details completed, *Wachusett* and her crew awaited the hour of attack. The details are in *Wachusett's* log:

> At 3 [a.m.] got under way from our anchorage and, under full head of steam struck the C.S. steamer *Florida* abaft the mizzen mast on the stbd side, crushing it in, carrying away the mizzen mast, & doing other serious damage. Some shots were exchanged with small arms and two shots were fired from our broadside guns. Upon being told to surrender, they replied that the Commander was on shore & also a number of their men. The officer then in command, Lt. T. Kennedy Porter, surrendered the vessel & boats were sent to take off prisoners. Actg. Masters Mate T. I. Graves succeeded in making fast a hawser to her & slipped her cable. We towed her to sea, being fired at with shell from the [Brazilian] forts in the harbor.[45]

Despite the laconic entries in the log, *Wachusett* gave *Florida* a near fatal blow. The unfortunate Porter later related that "she struck us abreast the mizzenmast, broke it into three pieces, crushed in the bulwarks, knocked the quarter boat in on deck, jammed the wheel, carried away the main yard and started the beams for about 30 feet forward."[46]

In tow of *Wachusett,* with her former crew clapped in irons below deck, *Florida* departed the harbor, fired upon by a Brazilian battery indignant over the violation of their sovereignty. After daylight a Brazilian warship in tow of a paddle gunboat was discovered following the two vessels but, aided by their sails, the pair escaped. However, the damage sustained by *Florida* made it necessary for her to be towed by *Wachusett* until 15 October. She had to be towed again from the 18th to the 21st, and again that same day until the following morning.

Stopping only once for provisions, *Wachusett* and her prize arrived at St. Thomas, in the Virgin Islands, on 30 October, where Collins found USS *Kearsarge*, whose crew perhaps relived their own victory over *Alabama* the previous June. The next day Collins commenced coaling, sending an officer home in *Kearsarge* with his report and "colors, swords &c." captured from *Florida*. The coaling, though necessary, turned into an embarrassment when, on the evening of 1 November, "at 8 p.m. 18 rebel prisoners effected their escape in a coal barge," eluding the deck watch, possibly overconfident after their victory.

Wachusett and her prize arrived at Hampton Roads in the late afternoon of 11 November. Twenty minutes after she anchored, "Capt. Collins was visited by the Admiral [Rear Admiral David D. Porter]." Admirals normally do not "visit" commanders without good reason and clearly Collins' actions had placed the Federal government in an embarrassing situation. The United States had gone to war with Great Britain in 1812 over the rights of neutrals; had endured the loss of *Essex* in a neutral country in that same war and, in this war, had been forced to return Confederate envoys taken from the British steamer *Trent* by USS *San Jacinto*. The Government's position was clearly weak. Even more mortifying, Brazil had been on friendly terms with the United States.

Nevertheless, the delivery from the threat of *Florida's* activities was secretly most welcome. Secretary of the Navy Gideon Welles summed up the situation:

> The Secretary of State has not known what to say, and, I think, not what to do. In our first or second conversation he expressed a hope that we should not be compelled to give up the *Florida*, and this he repeated in each of our subsequent interviews...That he owed a respectful apology to Brazil, I not only admitted but asserted. We have disturbed her peace, been guilty of discourtesy, etc., etc...I would make amends for her offended sovereignty by any proper acknowledgements. I do not believe she will have the impudence to ask restitution.[47]

However, Brazil did have the "impudence" to ask for restitution, and Collins was ordered to return *Florida* to Bahia, whereupon a suspiciously convenient "accident" intervened. Admiral Porter, who clearly was delighted to be rid of the troublesome raider, explained, "The expedition against Fort Fisher was then fitting out, and the [Hampton] Roads were crowded with vessels of every description. While the *Florida* was lying in the stream an army transport came in collision with her but did her no damage."[48] Porter's memory was highly selective. On 22 November 1864, his fleet captain had reported the steam transport *Alliance* "came athwart the *Florida*'s bow, carrying away the jib boom and figurehead. She then drifted alongside, carrying away the *Florida*'s cathead, hammock nettings, a portion of the port main rigging, boat davit and bumpkin."[49] Since the damage sustained when she was captured at Bahia had not been repaired, and she was leaking about five inches an hour, *Florida* was obviously unseaworthy and unfit for the return voyage.

Two decades later Porter explained his subsequent actions. "It was reported that the collision was intentional, and to avoid further accident Admiral Porter directed the *Florida* to be stripped of everything valuable, her guns taken out and the vessel moored securely head and stern at Newport News, just at the spot where the *Cumberland* was sunk in very deep water."*

On 24 November Porter did, in fact, give *Florida*'s commanding officer such an order but he concluded with the following cryptic sentence: "Be careful to carry out the instructions accompanying this."[50] A separate order giving detailed instructions as to housekeeping details did accompany the first order, but a lingering air

---

* Porter's memory was faulty, whether by accident or design. USS *Cumberland*, a sail sloop-of-war, had been rammed and sunk 8 March 1862 off Hampton Roads by CSS *Virginia*, formerly USS *Merrimack*, in the conflict that preceded the famous battle between USS *Monitor* and *Virginia* the following day. In point of fact, *Cumberland* actually went down in about fifty feet of water, her topmasts were above water, her commission pennant was still flying and efforts were made to salvage her.

of intrigue remains. Was there another separate order, written or oral? The answer will probably never be known, but Porter's glib explanation creates more doubts than it resolves:

> [B]ut, strangely enough, although the *Florida* was to all appearances water-tight when she reached Newport News, she sank that night at two o'clock in ten fathoms, and there she lay for some years after the war…. When the sinking of the vessel was reported to Admiral Porter, he merely said, 'Better so'; while the Secretary of State and Secretary of the Navy never asked any questions about the matter, being too well satisfied to get the elephant off their hands.[51]

At any event *Florida* was gone leaving but two matters to be disposed of: the question of disciplinary action against Collins, and reparations to Brazil. Both were handled with suspicious ease.

On 7 April 1865, just one week before the end of the war and with Union victory an assured fact, Collins was tried by a court martial on the charge of unlawfully attacking and capturing *Florida* in a neutral port. He pleaded guilty except for the word "unlawfully." In effect Collins admitted the facts but asserted by striking out the word "unlawfully" that his acts were justifiable. In view of this plea the prosecuting judge advocate offered no evidence, nor did Collins, who merely introduced a paper he had signed stating that his acts were "for the public good."*

The court found him guilty and ordered him dismissed from the service.[52] From a modern point of view, the proceedings are legally suspicious and the conviction could not stand up under review. It is highly likely that the court knew it would not stand up under Civil War standards either. This is substantiated by the fact that Collins was promoted to captain while the sentence was

---

* Modern practice requires that a defendant who pleads guilty must state the facts orally in open court, under oath and on the record. The plea itself is not deemed sufficient. Collins' plea would be entered as a plea of not guilty and the defendant would stand trial.

under review. No higher authority would promote a convicted officer without a pretty firm belief that such conviction would not stand.

Nearly a year and half later, the war over for the same period of time, *Florida* in her grave for almost two years, and Collins in the meantime promoted, Welles disapproved the sentence of the court martial and restored him to duty. No explanation was given nor would one appear necessary in view of the whole record. Collins was promoted to commodore on 19 January 1871 and rear admiral in 1874. He died the following year.

There still remained the difficulty with Brazil, whose sovereignty had been violated and whose grievance was justified. This problem was solved neatly with the acquiescence of Brazil, now confronted by a victorious and restored Union. On 23 July USS *Nipsic* lay in the harbor of Bahia dressed for the anniversary of the coronation of the Emperor of Brazil with the Brazilian flag at her main mast. At noon the American flag was hauled down from her foremast and the Brazilian flag raised in its place. A salute of twenty-one guns was fired, the salute being returned gun for gun by the Brazilian corvette *Dona Januaria*. This was accepted as a suitable apology, although Brazil never got back *Florida* or monetary reparations. Honor was thus deemed satisfied and the matter was closed, not at all a bad price to pay for the destruction of one of the Confederacy's most deadly weapons.

*   *   *

The incident is related fully in O.R.N. I, 3, 254-70. In addition, the deck log of *Wachusett* in the National Archives was consulted, as was the Diary of Gideon Welles.

CHAPTER XI

Raid of the Rebel Rams

The extent to which the Confederacy engaged in the production of armored vessels, called by both sides "ironclads" or "rams," is sometimes greatly underestimated. From start to finish, the South projected forty-six ironclads, all but five of the casemate design, exemplified by CSS *Virginia*, ex-USS *Merrimack*, which had been described by one man who fought her as resembling a house floating downstream. Of the forty-one casemated vessels proposed, the South was able to complete and commission the surprising number of twenty-one, although, fortunately for the Union, they were slow in completion, scattered in location, and generally deficient both in engines and armament.

The fate of these formidable vessels varied greatly. *Virginia* destroyed two Union wooden sailing vessels and crippled two more before she was stalemated by *Monitor* and blown up at the evacuation of Norfolk by the Confederates in 1862. In 1863, *Atlanta* surrendered after only three shots from one gun aboard her adversary, the monitor *Weehawken*,* although it took

---

* *Weehawken* actually carried two guns, an 11 and a 15 inch, but the fire from the 15 inch did the damage.

a whole fleet to bring down *Tennessee* at Mobile Bay in 1864. Both *Atlanta* and *Tennessee* were subsequently taken into the United States Navy and served against their former masters. *Albemarle,* after defeating a flotilla of wooden Union vessels, succumbed to a torpedo and sank at her berth in Plymouth, North Carolina, in 1864. Although later raised and taken to the Norfolk Navy Yard, she never served in the United States Navy. Most of the rest either were never finished, ran aground in the shallow waters of the Confederacy or were simply destroyed at their docks. The most potent threat by the Confederate rams lay in Charleston, South Carolina.

Chicora and *Palmetto State* were sisters, two of the six ship *Richmond* class, different only in relatively minor details of armament. Resembling *Virginia* except that they were some fifty feet shorter, they posed a considerable threat to the Federal forces from the time of their commissioning in the autumn of 1862. Although they never left Charleston during their entire service, they constituted an excellent example of a "fleet in being," since the Federals could never quite ignore the threat of their presence.

In a daring attempt to break the blockade of that harbor they sortied about four o'clock in the morning of 31 January 1863.

*　　*　　*

Charleston had been a thorn in the side of the Union since the beginning of the war. Although some of the Union's anger resulted from the firing on Fort Sumter and the beginning of the Civil War, the seaport possessed such natural advantages that the Union never could completely shut it down until the closing days of the war. Secretary of the Navy Gideon Welles irately placed it at the top of his list of targets, refusing almost to the end of the war to believe

CSS Albemarle, *a typical Confederate ironclad. Confederate armor plate sometimes had to be improvised from railroad tracks.*

naval force alone could not take it. To this end he assigned to the South Atlantic Blockading Squadron, under the command of Rear Admiral Samuel F. Du Pont, enough ships to draw the noose tightly around Charleston's neck. On January 31, 1863, Du Pont had fifteen ships, including *New Ironsides*, the most powerful warship in the world, on the blockade of Charleston. Unfortunately, *New Ironsides*, which had been expected to dispose easily of the Confederate ironclads *Chicora* and *Palmetto State*, had just departed for Port Royal for repairs.

Experienced officers commanded the iron sisters. In *Palmetto State* was Lieutenant Commander John Rutledge CSN, who had spent twenty-six years in the old navy, resigning his commission as lieutenant at the outbreak of the war. On board with him, Flag Officer Duncan S. Ingraham had served thirty-nine years in the old service. Commander John R. Parker was in *Chicora*; he had left the old navy with the rank of commander after thirty-five years.

Taking advantage of mild weather—only a slight breeze attended with a thick haze[1]—the ironclads stole down the harbor at midnight, then out through the main ship channel, looking for Federal men-of-war. They did not look long.

They first encountered USS *Mercedita,* a wooden-hulled 195-foot gunboat. Her recently promoted commander, Captain Henry S. Stellwagen, had spent a good part of the night on the bridge pursuing a suspicious vessel that turned out to be a stray Union troop transport. Stellwagen had just returned to his cabin, leaving the job of anchoring to his executive officer, Lieutenant Commander Trevett Abbot, and the officer of the deck, Acting Master Thomas J. Dwyer. Suddenly a commotion and a cry called him back on deck. "She has black smoke. Watch, man the guns, spring the rattle, call all hands to quarters."

Seeing smoke and "a low boat" which he mistook for a tug, Stellwagen ordered the guns made ready to fire and trained on the stranger, then hailed, "Steamer ahoy! Stand clear of us and heave to! What steamer is that?" An unintelligible "Halloo" followed by indistinct words was returned. The stranger did not stop but rammed the unfortunate *Mercedita* on her starboard quarter, while simultaneously discharging a seven-inch gun into her. By the time Stellwagen realized he had encountered *Palmetto State,* his adversary was too close—he could not fire his own guns against her.

Nor could Stellwagen maneuver his ship. That seven-inch shell fired into her had penetrated *Mercedita* diagonally from starboard to port, passed through the fresh water condenser and the steam drum of the port boiler, thus filling the ship with steam, and blown a hole over four feet square in the port side. Sheer pandemonium followed. Conflicting reports came almost simultaneously: "Shot though both boilers," "Fires put out by steam and water," "Gunner and one man killed," "Number of men fatally scalded," "Water over fire room floor," and, ominously, "Vessel sinking fast. The ram has cut us through at and below the water line on one side, and the shell has burst on the other about at the water's edge."

Palmetto State had turned under *Mercedita*'s starboard counter

and Ingraham hailed, "Surrender, or I'll sink you." The beleaguered Stellwagen replied, "I can make no resistance; my boiler is
destroyed." As he later put it, "I could bring nothing to bear but
muskets against his shot-proof coating."[2] Throwing his signal book
overboard, as was his duty to do, he surrendered.

Mercedita lowered a boat and Lieutenant Commander Abbot
went to the ironclad to "see what they demanded." He was escorted
to Captain Rutledge and advised him that *Mercedita* was sinking
with a crew of 158 aboard, that she was disabled, and that all the
ship's boats were full of water, having been lowered without inserting the drain plugs. Rutledge, in turn, reported this to Ingraham,
who now faced a dilemma: with *Chicora* engaged with another
vessel and *Palmetto State* cleared for action, Ingraham could not
take possession of the captured *Mercedita* with or without her crew.
Nor, with the latter's boats unusable, could he abandon her, scuttle
her, or set her on fire without condemning her crew to certain
death, an act tantamount to murder. Ingraham resorted to the next
best course; he offered to place *Mercedita* on parole. "At this time
the *Chicora* was engaged with the enemy and the alarm was given.
I knew our only opportunity was to take the enemy unawares, as
the moment he was underway, from his superior speed, we could
not close with him."[3]

The hapless Abbot was unable to refuse. Accordingly, he agreed
to "pledge my sacred word of honor that neither I nor any of the
officers and crew of the *Mercedita* would again take up arms against
the Confederate States during the war, unless legally and regularly
exchanged as prisoners of war."[4] Ingraham agreed to this pledge and
released Abbot to return to his own vessel. Nobody realized that while
the parole covered the entire ship's company of *Mercedita,* nothing
whatsoever was mentioned with respect to the vessel herself.

Abbot, returning to *Mercedita,* reported to Stellwagen, who accepted the parole as written and then set all hands to work repairing
the damage and getting his vessel ready to move. While the steam
drum of the port boiler had been destroyed, the starboard boiler was
intact, allowing the engine to be worked at a slow speed. *Mercedita* set

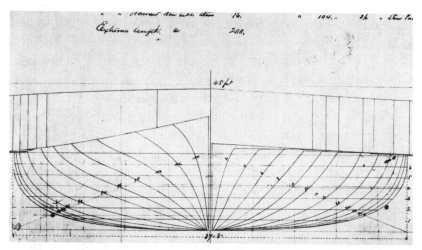

Hull plan, dating from 1862, of the Passaic *class ironclads, showing the characteristic shallow draft and wide deck. (Naval Historical Center, NH 42805)*

out for Port Royal, South Carolina, arriving late that same day. On board were thirteen of the crew who had fled *Mercedita* in a ship's boat, returning only when it was clear that she was neither going to sink nor be captured. They were not welcomed back.

While *Palmetto State* was working over *Mercedita*, *Chicora* engaged USS *Keystone State* further along the main ship channel. *Keystone State*, commanded by Commander William E. Le Roy, somewhat larger but considerably slower than *Mercedita*, had been built for coastal trade. As vulnerable to an ironclad as her companion, she at least was forewarned of the attack and resisted for more than an hour before she, too, succumbed.* Le Roy recorded his account in the log:

---

* Le Roy was so strongly affected by the battle that he dictated and signed additional remarks to the log—remarks so graphic that the compilers of the Official Records reproduced them in their chronicle of the engagement. They ought to be read in full. ORN I,13, 583.

On heading to the northward and eastward, discovered a ram on either quarter. Soon after the first gun [was fired], fire was reported forward, below. After extinguishing it, fire was soon again reported in the same place, when the ship was kept off seaward to enable us to put out the fire and get things in condition to attack the enemy. Ordered full steam, and about daylight discovered black smoke and stood for it for the purpose of running her down. Exchanged shots rapidly with her, striking her repeatedly but making no impression, while every shot from her was striking us.

About 6:17 a.m. a shell entering in the port side, forward of the forward guard, destroyed the steam chimneys, filling all the forward part of the ship with steam. The port boiler emptied of its contents, the ship gave a heel to starboard nearly down to the guard, and the water from the boiler and two shot holes under the water led to the impression that the ship was filling and sinking, a foot and a half of water being reported in the hold. Owing to the steam, men were unable to get ammunition from forward. Ordered all boats ready for lowering, signal book thrown overboard, and also some small arms.

The ram being so near and the ship being helpless and the men being slaughtered by almost every discharge of the enemy, I ordered the colors to be hauled down, but finding that the enemy was still firing on us I directed the colors to be rehoisted, and resumed our fire from the after battery.[5]

Lieutenant Commander Thomas H. Eastman, Le Roy's Executive Officer, wrote to his wife of the carnage:

Just as we got within 300 yards, going at the rate of 12 miles,* he put a shot through both our boilers and blew us up. Then we were done. The ship fell over on her side; she had four large holes in her bottom; we could not move any more and one fourth of our strong crew were killed or wounded. Captain Le Roy (God bless

---

* *Keystone State* was rated at 9.5 knots, Silverstone. *Warships of the Civil War*, Naval Institute Press, 1989, 73.

him), out of pity for the dying and the dead, hauled down our flag; the ironclad fired two more shot into us. Then Le Roy ran the flag up and we went to work at him [the ram] again.

Yesterday we buried our dead—23, probably 3 more tomorrow. At daylight that morning we mustered 196, now we muster 138 all told... We are all knocked to pieces, eleven (120-pounder) shell went into us and two burst on the quarter-deck.[6]

Tucker, in *Chicora*, gave another side of the story:

We then engaged...a large side-wheel steamer...causing her to strike her flag; at this time the latter vessel, supposed to be the *Keystone State*, was completely at my mercy, I having taken a position astern, distant some 200 yards. I at once gave the order to cease firing upon her, and directed Lieutenant [George H.] Bier, first lieutenant of the *Chicora*, to man a boat and take charge of the prize; if possible to save her; if that was not possible, to rescue her crew. While the boat was being manned I discovered that she was endeavoring to make her escape by working her starboard wheel, the other being disabled, her colors being down. She then hoisted her flag and commenced firing her rifled guns, her commander, by this faithless act, placing himself beyond the pale of civilized and honorable warfare. The *Keystone State* did not surrender, rescue or no rescue, and her escape ought probably to be regarded as a rescue.[7]

While Stellwagen, in *Mercedita*, limped into Port Royal unaided, Le Roy was unable to move at all under his own power and received a tow from the former blockade runner *Memphis*, now converted into a blockader. He arrived at Port Royal the following day to begin the task of repairing his ship and burying his dead.

Ingraham had inflicted grievous harm upon two of his enemies but, because of his inferior speed, had to forsake his mission of destroying the blockade. He and his consort returned to Charleston Harbor, while USS *Housatonic*, the only other vessel to see action at all, fired on them without effect. *New Ironsides* never even entered the action.

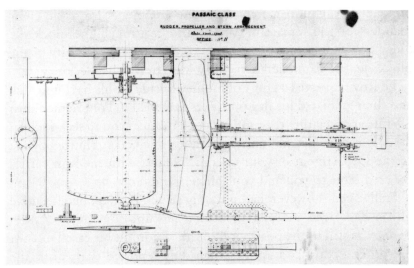

Plan of rudder, propeller and stern arrangement of Passaic *class iron-clads, from the original drawings of 1862. Similar to* Monitor, *this class also included USS* Lehigh, Montauk, *and* Weekawken. *(Naval Historical Center, NH 42804)*

The great raid was over but its aftermath was not. The Confederates took some of the foreign consuls to the harbor entrance in a tug, from which vantage point they failed to see (or reported that they failed to see, which is not quite the same thing) any Union blockaders. After some initial doubts, General Pierre G.T. Beauregard, the army ground commander, and Flag Officer Ingraham, the naval commander, issued a joint proclamation: Confederate naval forces had "attacked the United States blockading fleet off the harbor of the city of Charleston and sunk, dispersed, or drove off and out of sight for the time being the entire hostile fleet."[8]

Because of this and statements by a few foreign consuls, particularly the British, and Captain George W. Watson RN, commander of the British sloop of war *Petrel,* then lying in Charleston harbor, that they saw no blockaders, Confederate Secretary of State Judah P. Benjamin issued an official notice proclaiming the blockade broken. The Union merely obtained statements from the commanders of the remaining vessels and continued the blockade. Since no foreign power attempted to challenge the validity of the blockade, the Confederate strategy was effectively checkmated.

Le Roy requested a court of inquiry to rule on his having struck and then rehoisted his flag on *Keystone State*. Du Pont denied this: "While appreciating the motive which induces you to seek such an investigation, I deem it unnecessary, for the facts submitted by me to the Department of your unequal contest with the iron vessels are creditable to you and your officers and crew."[9]

Stellwagen, however, had not only struck his flag, his executive officer had given a parole for the entire ship's company, yet *Mercedita* was still in the possession of the Union! In his case Du Pont did order a court of inquiry which duly reported that, while the parole given did include the officers and crew, it did not include the vessel and its equipment. Du Pont forwarded the report to Welles with the endorsement that, although the court had recommended further military proceedings, presumably a court martial, for Stellwagen's alleged want of vigilance in detecting the raiders— even had Stellwagen anticipated the attack he could not have changed the outcome, as "the contest was too unequal." The thirteen would-be deserters were treated more harshly—they were confined and sent to Philadelphia with *Mercedita* when she went north for repairs.

Secretary Welles, who had exploded some four months earlier when CSS *Florida* had broken into Mobile Bay, had matured with the bitter experience of defeat. Having in January learned that not only had *Florida* broken out of Mobile, but CSS *Alabama* had engaged and sunk USS *Hatteras*, Welles merely remarked philosophically,

> We have the world agog with an account of an onset of our fleet before Charleston. The *Mercedita* is reported to have been surprised and sunk and other vessels damaged. But the general hullabaloo is over a report that the whole blockading fleet ran away—the foreign

In this poor quality but extremely rare picture, (from left) USS Weehawken, Montauk, *and* Passaic *bombard Confederate positions on Sulli-*
van's Island, South Carolina, 8 September 1863. Snapped by a
Confederate cameraman, this is the only known photograph of Civil War
ironclads in action. (Naval Historical Center, NH 51964)

consuls at Charleston went out and could see none of the vessels—
and the blockade is by the Rebels declared raised... Not unlikely
the *Mercedita* may have been surprised and sunk, as she is of light
draft and was probably close in. If there had been other vessels
captured or sunk, we should have had their names. It looked to me
as if the budget [story] was made up for the European market by
the foreign consuls, who are, in fact, Rebel agents.[10]

Although Welles declined to proceed any further against Stellwagen, he did not assign him to another steam vessel. Instead, he
exiled him to the Mediterranean in command of the sail frigate
Constellation, a veteran of the quasi war with France of 1799.
Stellwagen remained in command of that ancient relic until she

155

returned to the United States when the war was nearly over. He retired in December 1865 and died some six months later.

Le Roy fared somewhat better. Left in command of *Keystone State*, he continued to serve under Du Pont. He became a captain in 1866, a commodore in 1870 and a rear admiral in 1874. He retired in 1880 and died in 1888, no doubt with the memories of his duel with *Chicora* fresh in his mind.

Mercedita was reassigned as a cruiser in the Caribbean. Probably because the Navy Department was in some doubt as to her status she never returned to blockading duty. She survived the war, returned to the merchant service and, serving as a barge, was lost at sea in 1901.

CHAPTER XII

Death in Galveston Harbor

Early in the morning of January 1, 1863, a fierce Confederate attack wrested the city of Galveston, Texas, from the control of Union forces and restored it to the Confederacy. Despite the decisive Union defeat, the battle was by no means one sided, and in that violent, desperate struggle either side might well have prevailed. The attack succeeded only because of the unlucky elimination of a very few pivotal officers at a crucial time.

*   *   *

The city of Galveston lies at the east end of Galveston Island, a barrier island some thirty miles long, connected to the mainland by a railroad causeway to the west of the city. To its north, separated by Galveston Channel, lies Pelican Island, surrounded by extensive marshy flats. To the northeast, across Bolivar Channel leading towards Houston, is Bolivar Point. The channel to the open sea runs from Bolivar Channel in a general southeasterly direction across a shallow bar, navigable only at high tide. The five-mile-long Galveston Channel and harbor lie between Galveston and Pelican Islands.

Galveston was the first major port west of New Orleans and it was crucial to the Confederate forces west of the Mississippi River. It had been in Confederate hands from the beginning of the war until October 4, 1862, when a Union naval expedition, comprising the steam gunboats *Westfield, Harriet Lane, Owasco,* and *Clifton*

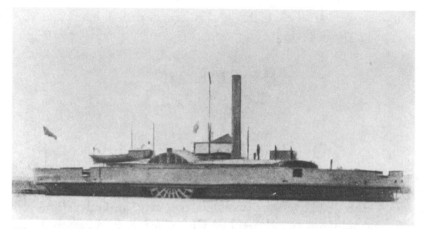

The armored ferryboat McDonough, *similar to those used by the Union at Galveston.*

and the schooner *Henry James* captured the city and island after a ridiculously feeble defense.

Although the navy had taken the island, area commander Rear Admiral David G. Farragut recognized that the Union could not hold it without troops to garrison it. However, Major General Benjamin F. Butler, the Union army commander, was unable or unwilling to supply the needed troops and sent to Galveston only Companies G, D, and I of the Forty-second Massachusetts Volunteers, some 260 men in all. Butler's successor, Major General Nathaniel P. Banks, had managed to scrape together additional reinforcements, but these were still en route to Galveston when the city fell, and were recalled just in time to escape capture.

To hold the island Farragut retained the vessels which had captured it, sending such supplies and support vessels as he could spare. The largest was the flagship, the side wheel steamer *Westfield,* under the command of Commander William B. Renshaw, the senior officer. *Westfield* was a converted Staten Island ferry boat, 250 feet long and heavily armed. Unfortunately, she drew the most water, which proved critical in the shallow waters of Galveston Bay.

The most powerful ship, the heavily armed paddle wheel steamer *Harriet Lane,* was brigantine rigged and able to travel under sail alone if need be. She had been built in 1857 as a revenue cutter and named for the niece of President James Buchanan. The navy took her over at the outbreak of the war, and she had fired the first naval shots of the war at Fort Sumter on 12 April 1861. *Harriet Lane's* captain was Commander Jonathan M. Wainwright and her executive officer Lieutenant Commander Edward Lea. Probably because of her three 9 inch guns, Renshaw positioned *Harriet Lane* nearest the enemy at the west end of the harbor.

Resembling *Westfield,* the converted ferry boat *Clifton,* commanded by Lieutenant Commander Richard L. Law, lay between *Harriet Lane* and *Westfield,* some distance from both. The gunboat *Owasco,* with one 11-inch and two 24-pounder smooth bore guns rounded out the roster of steam warships—the only ones that really mattered in this first of modern wars. However, there were other Union ships present, including the schooner *Corypheus,* the screw steamer *Sachem,* the captured blockade runner *Velocity* and some coal schooners. These ships, which had gained the port so heroically and were to lose it so spectacularly, might have been adequate had they been differently employed, but Renshaw's disposition of his vessels proved to be unfortunate. *Harriet Lane* lay anchored at the west end of the harbor, nearest the expected Confederate attack, some distance from *Clifton* and several miles from *Westfield.* If the enemy attacked from that direction, *Lane* would be the prime target, with no assistance readily available and the flagship too remote to provide aid.

Harriet Lane's executive officer, Lieutenant Commander Edward Lea, had had a good year. He had fought with the fleet of Flag Officer, now Rear Admiral, Farragut; with the fleet he had driven thirty miles up the Mississippi River to Confederate Forts St. Philip and Jackson, had run past those forts to the capture of New Orleans; had seen service with the mortar flotilla of Commander David D. Porter, and earned his appointment as Executive Officer of *Harriet Lane.* Now he and his companions had captured

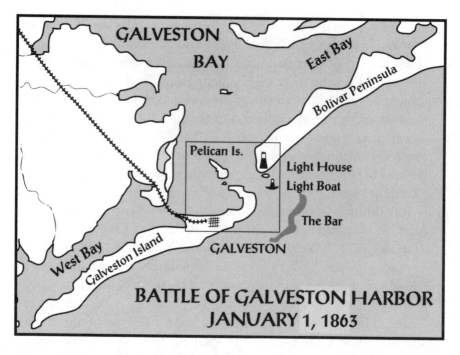

GALVESTON BAY

East Bay

Bolivar Peninsula

Pelican Is.

Light House

Light Boat

The Bar

West Bay

Galveston Island

GALVESTON

**BATTLE OF GALVESTON HARBOR
JANUARY 1, 1863**

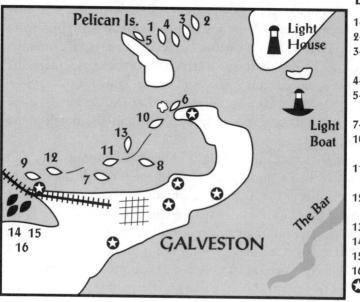

Pelican Is.

Light House

Light Boat

The Bar

GALVESTON

LEGEND

1-USS Westfield
2-USS Saxon
3-USS M.A.
   Boardman
4-USS Velocity
5-,6-Coal
   steamers
7-USS Sachem
10-USS Owasco,
   intitial position
11-USS Owasco,
   engaging batteries
12-USS Owasco,
   aground
13-USS Clifton
14-CSS Bayou City
15-CSS Neptune
16-CSS John F. Carr
☆-Forts/batteries

Galveston, Texas. Nevertheless, Lea was engaged in civil war and the enemy was not a foreign invader but his own countrymen—in fact, his own family. Edward Lea's father, A.M. Lea, was a major in the Confederate army and a member of the staff of Major General J. Bankhead Magruder, the commander of the Confederate forces confronting the Federals in Galveston.

31 December had been peaceful, although there had been rumors of an impending Confederate attack. *Owasco*, having spent the afternoon coaling, anchored off Pelican Spit some three miles or more east of *Harriet Lane* and occupied herself with condensing fresh water. Save for somewhat more breeze than might be desirable on a winter's evening, all seemed as it had on previous nights; this tranquility was deceptive, however. Half an hour before midnight the Confederate cavalry drove in the pickets of the Union army troops garrisoned in the town. An hour and a half later the Union troops reported enemy artillery in the market place. Nonetheless, it was 1:30 a.m. before a preparatory signal, the first indication of trouble, was made from the troops ashore. At almost the same moment, both *Clifton* and *Westfield* discovered "some two or three rebel steamers" in the bay above *Clifton*. This marked the commencement of the battle, although three o'clock seems to be the time when the real action commenced. At that time the Confederate land forces attacked the Massachusetts troops, the Federals forming behind barricades at their headquarters on Kuhn's Wharf. Both the Confederate infantry and artillery attacked these barricades together and the fire fight continued until daylight.

About this time Renshaw, who was furthest from the scene, got *Westfield* under way to join the action. Unfortunately, he ran her so hard aground on the northeast side of Pelican Spit that, despite the aid of *Clifton*, which had steamed to her assistance instead of heading for the scene of action, she remained immobilized. Thus, two of the most powerful Union vessels remained several miles from the action, a fatal reduction in the Federal force.

Sometime between three and five o'clock the brightly shining moon went down, leaving behind a dark haze. The extremely poor visibility was just the opportunity the Confederates had been waiting for, and they launched their attack from west to east down Galveston Channel.

Two Confederate vessels, the *Bayou City*, a Houston and Galveston packet commanded by Captain Henry Lubbock, and the *Neptune*, a similar vessel commanded by Major Leon Smith, led the attack. Smith, a former merchant captain and army officer, headed the expedition. More than a hundred men, protected against small arms fire by bulwarks of cotton bales, manned each vessel and sharpshooters from Texas cavalry regiments fortified each boat. *Bayou City* boasted a 32 pounder rifled gun and *Neptune* two howitzers. The pair had laid up at Halfmoon Shoals about fifteen miles from Galveston, awaiting the signal for attack. Approximately half an hour after the moon had set they went into activity when, the shore guns having commenced firing at the Federal troops, Smith ordered them to advance "with all the steam we could crack on." Followed by the steamer *John F. Carr* and with their furnaces fired with rosin to produce a hotter flame, the little flotilla pushed rapidly towards Galveston. At about 5:30 the *Harriet Lane* opened fire on them while the remaining Union vessels engaged the shore batteries in support of the Massachusetts troops on shore. The pivotal part of the battle had begun.

The next half hour was a melee, which determined the outcome of the struggle, during which the Federal forces fought bravely and well. The Confederate *Bayou City* and *Neptune* went directly for *Harriet Lane*, *Bayou City* firing her 32 pounder as she drove at her target. Unfortunately her gun burst at the third round, killing the gun captain and wounding several others. *Harriet Lane* gave as good as she got, ramming *Bayou City* and tearing off part of the port wheelhouse and side. Not content with this, *Lane* then rammed into *Neptune*, disabling her so badly that she backed into shoal water and sank. *Bayou City* then turned into *Harriet Lane*, catching under her wheel guard and pinning the two vessels together. Now the Confederate preparations paid off. Concealed behind their cotton bulwarks, the sharpshooters zeroed in on the

Magruder's Confederates storm aboard USS Harriet Lane *during the engagement in Galveston Harbor.*

exposed decks of *Harriet Lane.* Panic, magnified by the noise and darkness, ensued on board the unfortunate warship, culminating in the manner of the old fashioned frigate actions of the War of 1812 when the Confederates, led by the audacious Smith, boarded the beleaguered vessel.

A short but bitter hand-to-hand combat followed, during which *Lane* suffered most, if not all, of her casualties. In what a Galveston newspaper tastelessly described as the *spolia optima,* or greatest triumph, Smith drove relentlessly towards *Lane's* officers. Spotting the wounded Commander Wainwright, whose body was already lacerated by three musket wounds in his left breast and three in his left thigh, Smith put a musket ball through his brain. Lieutenant Commander Lea also fell, mortally wounded from five wounds in his abdomen and side. As Lea lay dying on the deck of *Harriet*

Lane, he was found by his father, who had boarded *Lane* as soon as possible to search for his son. There was time for a brief reconciliation before Edward Lea expired in his father's arms.

Two other officers, Acting Masters Charles H. Hamilton and Willis F. Monroe, the Master at Arms, G.W. Davis and Boatswain's Mate William Ray, were all also wounded, Monroe fatally. Thus *Lane*'s six killed and fifteen wounded included her principal executive officers, the ship's disciplinarian, and one of her crucial petty officers. The demoralized crew surrendered *Lane*, whereupon she was immediately fired upon by *Owasco*, whose captain, Wilson, kept his composure.

Smith's daring and successful boarding set the stage for one of the most brazen deceptions of the war. Having possession only of the crippled *Lane*, with one of his own ships sunk and the other damaged, still confronted by the undamaged *Owasco*, *Clifton*, *Corypheus* and, so far as he knew, *Westfield*, Smith hoisted the white flag of truce. Flags of truce are rarely seen in modern times, but they were in frequent use during the Civil War, halting any fighting in areas where the flag was visible.

The results were dramatic. The flag of truce was promptly repeated by *Owasco*, *Clifton* and *Corypheus*, all of which ceased firing. The Federal troops on shore also ceased firing and raised a flag of truce at the same time, setting the stage for Smith to send a small boat with one of his own officers and one of the surviving Union officers from *Harriet Lane* to *Clifton*, which by then had anchored near *Owasco*. That emissary reported to Law, *Clifton*'s commander, that Wainwright and Lea had been killed and, falsely, that two-thirds of *Lane*'s crew had been wounded. Smith boldly claimed all Union vessels as prizes and offered to allow one of them to depart with the crews of all vessels.

To this brash and unenforceable demand, Law, who, like the rest of the Federal commanders, seems to have been bemused by the flag of truce, replied somewhat lamely that he had no authority to make such a decision, but offered to accompany the Confederate emissary and the injured Union officer to Renshaw on *Westfield*, still aground far away on Pelican Spit. As he left his own ship, Law ordered *Owasco* to cease firing and this order was obeyed by her. During the passage from *Clifton* to *Westfield* and while the flags of truce were still flying, the Confederates proceeded without opposition to make prisoners of the unfortunate Massachusetts troops, whose disillusionment at the debacle afloat must have been great, since at that time they had suffered but one man wounded and none killed.

When the flag of truce arrived aboard *Westfield*, still hard aground, Renshaw declined to surrender. However, instead of rallying the remaining vessels and continuing the struggle, he instructed Law to return to his own ship and get all Union vessels out of port as soon as possible. Renshaw further advised Law that, since he could not get *Westfield* afloat, he would blow her up and take his officers and crew aboard the army transports *Saxon* and *M. A. Boardman* lying nearby. Law at once began to carry out his orders while Renshaw set about on the destruction of his flagship.

Law first ordered Acting Master Alden T. Spear, commanding *Corypheus*, to spike his guns, burn his vessel and take to his ship's boats for Bolivar Channel. Spear countered with a request to take *Corypheus* out, which Law granted if *Corypheus*—a sailing vessel, with no steam power to aid her—"could stand it to pass the batteries." Law stipulated, however, that Spear must wait until the flags of truce had been hauled down before he escaped, a nicety not followed by the Confederates.

Meanwhile, Renshaw set about the destruction of his command. Rejecting the protests of his own and other officers, both army and navy, he evacuated his crew and laid a train of turpentine from the *Westfield*'s deck to her magazine. With his boat's crew lying alongside her, Renshaw applied the torch to *Westfield* with his own hands. It was his last act on this earth, for *Westfield* immediately blew up, instantly killing Renshaw and all his boat's crew and destroying the forward half of the vessel. The explosion, while rendering *Westfield* a useless wreck, did not damage her after end, nor did it destroy her guns, which were almost immediately raised by the Confederates and placed in service against their former owners.

If there had been any doubt about the completeness of the Confederate victory, the explosive destruction of *Westfield* resolved it. Law, in *Clifton*, hauled down the flag of truce and led the defeated Federals, not only out of the harbor and across the bar, but all the way to New Orleans to report to Farragut.* The following day in the Episcopal cemetery of Galveston the grieving Major Lea conducted a Masonic burial service over the common grave of Wainwright and Lea. Ironically, on the day of the battle, as Lea lay dying on the deck of *Harriet Lane*, Admiral Farragut in New Orleans signed an order detaching Lea from *Harriet Lane* and ordering him to New Orleans for the command of a mortar boat flotilla, with his own flagship to be designated on his arrival.

Farragut, when he heard of the disaster, exploded: "I can not think but that for the death of Commander Wainwright and Lieutenant Commander Lea the vessel would not have been surrendered. It is difficult, however, to conceive a more pusillanimous surrender of a vessel to an enemy already in our power than occurred in the case of the *Harriet Lane*." He ordered a court of inquiry to make a complete investigation.

Law was tried by court martial on two charges: failure to do his utmost to capture or destroy a vessel which it was his duty to encounter (*Harriet Lane*) and leaving his station and going to New Orleans in time of war before being regularly relieved. He was convicted on both counts and sentenced to be dismissed from the Navy. The court recommended clemency, however, because of his

---

* Law's failure to leave a guard vessel led to unfortunate consequences. Two days after his departure, the Union transport *Cambria* arrived off Galveston Bar with several hundred reinforcements for the Union garrison. After a yawl boat under the command of one Thomas Smith, a citizen of Galveston who had deserted from the Confederate army, was sent in for a pilot, the transport smelled a rat and hastily departed, abandoning the unfortunate Smith to his fate. He was captured, tried as a deserter and immediately shot.

prior gallant service and praise he had received from Farragut for his conduct prior to the Galveston battle. President Lincoln modified the sentence from dismissal to suspension from rank and duty for three years, the first six months to be without pay. This reduction seems equitable: Renshaw, not Law, was in command, and it was Renshaw's, not Law's, decision to evacuate Galveston. If there is any blame, it must attach to Renshaw for his initial disposition of his vessels and his insistence on destroying *Westfield*. However, Renshaw paid for these errors with his life, and he and his ship should be permitted to rest in peace. Law remained in the service, being promoted to commander in 1866 and captain in 1877. He was placed on the retired list in 1886 and died in 1891.

Wilson, in *Owasco*, seems to have been regarded as having done somewhat less than he should, having fired only 128 shots from all his guns during a five hour battle, hardly a lively barrage and the board of inquiry criticized "the failure of the *Owasco*" during the battle. While Wilson was retained in command, he was not promoted to commander until 1867 nor to captain until 1878. He died in 1894, three years after Law.

Farragut sent a letter of commendation to Acting Master Spear of *Corypheus*, who had stood up to Law and escaped with his ship, promoted five of his crew and recommended him for promotion. The Navy Department concurred and, on 19 February 1863, Farragut forwarded Spear a promotion to acting volunteer lieutenant:

> I herewith have the pleasure of forwarding to you your appointment as an acting volunteer lieutenant for the faithful performance of your duty under the most trying circumstances, when you had neither example nor authority to support you, but, on the contrary, both calling on you to betray that trust which your Government had reposed in you when it bestowed on you your original appointment; and hoping that you will never forget those inestimable words, "Reposing special trust and confidence in the patriotism, valor, fidelity, and abilities, I do appoint you as an officer in the Navy."

The old admiral's courtly praise must certainly have encouraged Spear, but did him little good otherwise; he died September 18, 1863, merely seven months and one day later. The cause of his death is not recorded.

Despite Federal fears that *Harriet Lane* would prove as dreaded a commerce raider as *Alabama* or *Florida,* her captor, Smith, could not get her to sea at all and she became the subject of a bitter jurisdictional dispute between the Confederate army and navy. She eventually became a blockade runner and made one trip to Havana, where she lay at the war's end. Sold into private service, she was eventually lost at sea.

The United States Navy has a tradition of naming combat vessels for naval heroes and it has, over the years, commemorated some of those who fought at Galveston. The Wainwright family has produced no less than five distinguished naval officers, as many as any family in the history of the Republic: Destroyers 62 and 419, as well as Destroyer Leader 28, have all born the name *Wainwright* commemorating the unfortunate Commander Wainwright; his son, Master Jonathan Wainwright, Jr., who died of wounds at San Blas, Mexico, in 1872; his cousin, Commander Richard Wainwright, who had died of wounds on August 10, 1862; *his* son, Rear Admiral Richard Wainwright and *his* son, Commander Richard Wainwright. During the Civil War a captured schooner was named in honor of Commander Renshaw and, in more modern times, destroyers 175 and 499 were likewise named for him. Destroyer 118 was commissioned in 1918 and served in both world wars under the name *Lea;* her service in the Second World War was as distinguished as that of her namesake. No United States warship has ever again born the name *Harriet Lane,* although the revenue service did continue it.

*   *   *

The entire Galveston story appears in O.R.N. I, 19, the taking by the Federals at pp. 253-263 and the retaking by the Confederates at pp. 437-477. References to it and the status of *Harriet Lane* appear scattered in the rest of Volume 19 and in Volume 20. The only deck log in the National Archives is that of *Owasco*. That of *Westfield* was most probably destroyed when she blew up, but why *Clifton* or *Corypheus* did not file theirs cannot be explained. Perhaps that of *Harriet Lane* is with her papers, returned at the end of the war but, so far, they seem not to have been located.

*   *   *

One cannot compare the modern chart of Galveston Harbor with that in the report of the Court of Inquiry (O.R.N. I, 19, 450) and not wonder whether the wrecks shown on the modern chart off the Northeast coast of Pelican Island might not indeed be those of *Westfield* and the coal schooners mentioned in the reports. Does she still lay there in her grave, the final relic of that fateful day?

CHAPTER XIII

The Cutting Out of the *Caleb Cushing*

When the good citizens of Portland, Maine, awoke in the morning of 27 June 1863, they discovered that the Civil War was at their front door. During the night, members of the Confederate Navy had infiltrated their harbor, taken by force the United States revenue cutter *Caleb Cushing*, and disappeared with their prize into the morning mist. Painful as the event may have been, however, it was the lancing of a boil for the Navy Department and many prominent Union politicians, since it ended the career of one of the more annoying rebel raiders, the bark *Tacony*, step-daughter of the legendary raider *Florida*.

The episode had its inception more than five months earlier and some fifteen hundred miles to the southwest, when Commander John Newland Maffitt CSN took *Florida* out of Mobile Bay past a Union blockading squadron, and into the Gulf of Mexico on a commerce raiding cruise. That escape on 16 January 1863 was the genesis of a series of losses to the Federal merchant marine which played havoc with the economy of the North and caused Secretary of the Navy Gideon Welles no end of grief.

*   *   *

On 6 May during the course of her commerce raiding, *Florida* captured the brig *Clarence* bound from Rio de Janeiro to Baltimore with a cargo of coffee. One of Maffitt's officers, Second Lieutenant Charles W. Read, proposed to Maffitt that he be allowed to take *Clarence*, with her cargo and papers intact, to Hampton Roads, Virginia, and either cut out a gunboat or burn the merchant vessels congregated there.[1] Maffitt acceded to this bold and risky plan and placed Read in command of *Clarence* with a crew of twenty men and one other officer, Third Assistant Engineer Eugene H. Brown. Arrangements were made for Maffitt to take *Florida* along the New England coast to meet them, and the two vessels separated that same day.

Read took *Clarence* North towards the Chesapeake. He must have been disappointed with his new command, for he related that he lost several vessels he chased because of her inferior sailing qualities. He was finally crowned with success when he captured the bark *Windward* on 6 June, the schooner *Alfred H. Partridge* on 7 June and the brig *Mary Alvina* on 9 June. From the latter two vessels he obtained information which convinced him that it would be foolhardy to attempt a raid on Hampton Roads. He accordingly determined to abandon this plan and act on his own initiative. (This was undoubtedly the correct decision; in Hampton Roads and the Norfolk area was the largest concentration of naval power on the continent; Read and his company would have been ground to powder by the angry Federals.)

Accordingly, Read headed *Clarence* north along the Atlantic coast in an effort to pick up further ships before his expected rendezvous with Maffitt. On June 12 he captured the bark *Tacony* bound in ballast to Philadelphia. Liking her more than he did the hapless *Clarence*, he determined to transfer to her and burn the slower vessel. While he was in the act of transferring the lone howitzer which was his armament, he picked up the schooner *Kate Stewart* off Cape Henry, Virginia, transferred some fifty prisoners to her and released her under bond. A period of relative prosperity now set in.

In twelve days Read captured sixteen vessels, varying from old fishing schooners to the ship *Isaac Webb,* carrying 750 passengers from Liverpool to New York. On 25 June, being for some reason dissatisfied with *Tacony,* Read burned her and transferred to the schooner *Archer.*

The release of *Kate Stewart* triggered a massive effort to hunt *Tacony* down and destroy her. Making for Philadelphia (although she had been within eight miles of Cape Henry when captured and could easily have gone into Hampton Roads when released), she paused long enough off the Cohansey River in the Delaware Bay to put William G. Mundy, late master of the *Tacony,* ashore at Greenwich, New Jersey, to travel overland to Philadelphia with the tidings that Read was on the loose. *Stewart's* owners lost no time in contacting Secretary of the Navy Gideon Welles.

There then ensued a frenzy of activity in an effort to contain the elusive raider. That same day Welles telegraphed Rear Admirals S.P. Lee at Newport News, Hiram Paulding at the New York Navy Yard, and Commodore Cornelius K. Stribling at the Philadelphia Navy Yard, and directing anything available to depart at once in search of *Tacony.* On the following day he directed Paulding, Stribling and Commodore John B. Montgomery at the Boston Navy Yard to "charter or seize half a dozen moderate-sized vessels; put on board an officer, a dozen men, plenty of small arms, and one or two howitzers; send them out in various directions."[2]

The officers involved reacted with commendable speed. Before the affair was over, involved were some forty chase vessels ranging from the famous schooner yacht *America* (which had been raised from the mud of a Florida river to be commissioned as a warship) to *Sabine,* the largest sail frigate in the United States Navy. Even the Treasury Department got in the act on 14 June when President Abraham Lincoln directed Secretary of the Treasury Salmon P. Chase to use his revenue cutters to cooperate with the navy, and that same day Secretary Chase ordered the revenue cutter *Cuyahoga* at New York to put to sea in pursuit of the raider.

Secretary Welles was besieged with calls, letters, and telegrams

The crew of the frigate Osliaba, *part of the Russian fleet which anchored in New York harbor during the Civil War. With many European governments sympathetic to the Confederacy, the U.S. government of the day greatly valued this display of Russian support.*

from national and local politicians and the marine insurance industry. Thus, he was appealed to by Nesmith and Sons, New York, Hon. A. A. Low, president of the New York Chamber of Commerce, A. Hardy & Co., Boston,[3] and a petition from the merchants of Boston to name but a few. Welles could probably empathize with these merchants as he was a Connecticut man himself, but he could hardly have been as sympathetic towards the politicians, some of whom thought they had the clout to affect his actions. One of these was United States Senator Edwin D. Morgan, formerly the governor of New York, who soon became active beyond the bounds of ordinary courtesy. On June 22, he wrote Welles from New York City,

> If the *Roanoke* is not going to sea immediately, I greatly desire that Admiral Paulding may be directed by the Navy Department to place her in a position to defend this harbor from attack by a hostile ship or steamer. I shall go to the Navy Yard to get information as to the condition of iron vessels there that can be used in case of emergency.[4]

USS *Roanoke* was a steam frigate, a sister ship of the late *Merrimack*, which had been converted by the Confederates to an ironclad and under the name of *Virginia* had fought to a draw with USS *Monitor* at Hampton Roads on 9 March 1862. *Roanoke* had been cut down in the same manner and given iron armor, differing, however, from *Virginia* in that she had *three* turrets, *Monitor* style, instead of her deceased sister's slab-sided casemate. The three turret design proved less than satisfactory during trials, and, in fact, she did spend a large part of her career protecting the port of New York. At the time, however, she was considered quite formidable, and Welles had plans to use her in the Norfolk-James River area. The decision as to her employment properly belonged to the Navy Department, not to a United States senator. However, such political intrusions were, and probably are, not unknown to the military. The following day Morgan wrote again:

> We have thought it not impossible that some of the Government ironclads might be spared for defending the harbor of New York. Our people are uneasy at the boldness of the pirates, and they will not rest much longer without efforts for more adequate protection for this harbor.
> On the 22nd instant I wrote you with relation to the frigate *Roanoke*, and hope to hear that she can now be spared for the defense of the port of New York.

The good secretary must have gnashed his teeth at this letter but he stuck to his guns and advised Morgan that (1) there were no ironclads available and (2) *Roanoke* was under orders to Norfolk.

Welles, after all, was a politician himself and could probably tolerate this type of pressure better than the telegram he received on the 27th from Major General John E. Wool from New York, who had already distinguished himself for his interference with naval affairs:

> The great ironclad steamer *Roanoke* ought not be taken from this great emporium from which you are supplied with money and almost everything to carry on the war against the rebels. The militia, as well as all the troops except about 700 are ordered elsewhere. To take the *Roanoke* from this city at the present moment will produce a very great excitement from all classes, friends as well as foes.

Obviously, Major General Wool did not believe in proper military channels. Earlier in the war, as commanding general of the Department of Virginia, he had not only failed to demonstrate any great desire to cooperate with the navy but had flatly refused to turn the recaptured Norfolk Navy Yard back to the Navy Department without a direct order from the Secretary of War.[5] Undaunted by Welles' attitude, he again wrote Welles on the 28th:

> I telegraphed you last night in relation to the retention in this port of the ironclad steamer *Roanoke*. In reply, you say that your orders in relation to her future disposition can not be revoked. I regret to learn this, for since then I have examined the navy yard. There is, save the *Roanoke* no vessel that will be fit for service under some ten days. I again repeat that this great emporium, from which both Army and Navy receive their supplies, as well as pay, ought not to be left without means of defense. The volunteers and militia of this city are being sent to Pennsylvania [this was within one week of the Battle of Gettysburg] to aid in the defense of that State. We shall be at the mercy of any privateers that may think it proper to assail this city. The temptation is indeed great, for the want of men to man the guns in the forts of the harbor.

P.S. I was accompanied in my visit to the navy yard by Ex-Governor Morgan, now U. S. Senator.

A more naked exercise of political pressure would be hard to find. Welles, however, had Wool down pat:

General Wool, Governor Morgan and Mayor Opdyke make a combined effort to retain the *Roanoke* at New York, and write me most earnestly on the subject. The idea that New York is in danger is an absurdity and, with a naval force always at the navy yard and in the harbor, and with forts and military force, is such a remote contingency that the most timid lady need not be, and is not, alarmed. Morgan and Opdyke, Governor and Mayor, have responsibilities that are perhaps excusable, but not General Wool, who feeds on panic and fosters excitement.[6]

He refused to budge, leaving the plans for *Roanoke* unaltered. Confronted with offers placing merchant vessels at his disposal for the chase of *Tacony*, and no doubt glad to get them, Welles still insisted that they be under naval command despite the shortage of trained naval officers available. He solved this by the ingenious method of ordering the navy yard commanders to have the respective merchant captains commissioned as acting masters without pay, thus giving the vessels some status as United States vessels and ratifying any actions they might take. At the same time, however, the Federal payroll was not encumbered nor was there any chance of untrained persons becoming professional naval officers.[7]

Despite the large number of vessels engaged in searching for him, Read avoided discovery until the morning of 26 June, when he entered the harbor of Portland, Maine. The previous day he had picked up two fishermen who, mistaking *Archer* for a pleasure yacht notwithstanding that she was a fishing schooner, agreed to pilot him into Portland. From these credulous dupes, Read learned that the revenue cutter *Caleb Cushing* was in the harbor, and that the passenger steamer to New York would remain in the harbor during the night. He determined to seize them for the Confederate

Commodore Perry, *one of numerous New York ferryboats armed and armored and pressed into Federal service. Their light draught and wide decks gave them a structure similar to the monitors.*

cause and accordingly took *Archer* into the harbor at sunset, boldly anchoring in full view of the shipping.

The cutter *Caleb Cushing* was a schooner one hundred feet in length, one of a class of four built in Massachusetts for the revenue service in 1853. Like the great majority of revenue cutters, she depended on sail alone for propulsion. (At the outset of the war only one revenue cutter, *Harriet Lane*, was a steam vessel and she had been turned over to the Navy Department before war broke out.[8]) *Cushing* lay at anchor in Portland harbor under the command of her first lieutenant, Dudley Davenport, her commanding officer having died of a heart attack earlier that day.

About one o'clock in the morning of 27 June, the watch on deck heard boats approaching and called Davenport, but before he could take the deck, the cutter was boarded from both sides, and he and the watch on deck were overpowered and put in irons. The takeover was complete; it only remained to make sail and get out of the harbor. That task, however, was not as simple as it seemed. There was no wind and no sailing vessel could move without wind. In fact, Read could not even slip the cable and had to raise the anchor by hand. It took the better part of an hour before *Cushing* was able to move at all, and then only by putting out two boats and towing the cumbersome cutter. Read's ideas of stealing the steamer were either forgotten or abandoned, a fact he must have regretted later on.

At eight in the morning, Jedediah Jewett, Collector of Customs for Portland, was advised that *Cushing* had departed the harbor and was to be seen about five miles off, standing for the open sea. Without full knowledge of the facts, Jewett initially put the blame on the unfortunate Davenport, who at the time, was in irons in his own cabin. Regardless of the blame, however, Jewett was a man of decision. Without waiting for orders from Secretary Chase, he at once went into action to recapture the stolen cutter.

He forthwith sent messengers to Fort Preble for guns and men of the Seventeenth Regulars, and to Colonel Edwin C. Mason of the Seventh Maine Volunteers at nearby Camp Lincoln, seeking similar assistance. While waiting, he began to round up the shipping to transport them. In this he was remarkably successful. Almost at once he chartered a 700 ton side-wheel steamer, the *Forest City*, the side-wheel steamer *Casco*, a steam tug, and obtained the services of the propeller steamer *Chesapeake*.

Chesapeake was the Portland-New York overnight steamboat that Read had originally intended to capture. She had been getting up steam for her departure to New York when Jewett descended on her, followed by Colonel Mason and the largest portion of his command, to which was added two 6 pound brass cannon from the state arsenal. The remainder of the troops were loaded on the other steamers; *Forest City* took on two 12 pounder field guns, thirty-five soldiers, forty muskets, and Lieutenant James H. Merryman of the Revenue Service, who arrived in town at four a.m., learned of the cutting out, and jumped aboard *Forest City* just as she was leaving the pier.

All took off in pursuit of the hapless Read within fifty minutes of the time Jewett learned of the theft, truly a remarkable piece of work on the collector's part. At the time *Cushing* was still only about ten miles off and beating to the westward out of Casco Bay. Her average speed was just about one mile per hour, a rate which must have seemed like eternity itself to Read and his men.

The convoy of steamers was discovered about ten o'clock by the men on *Cushing*. The cutter was cleared for action, a move which promptly taught Read the predicament he was in. Any armament which he may have brought with him was, of course, left on *Archer* when he took *Cushing*. (He does not mention whether he transferred the howitzer, which Maffitt gave him, from *Tacony* to *Archer* but it proved academic, because he did not take it with him when he cut out *Cushing* and thus was dependent on whatever armament the cutter had been supplied with.)

This should have been sufficient, and probably would have been, had Read made better use of the eight hour start he had been given to put the cutter in a defensible state. When he finally turned his attention to defense, he discovered that *Cushing* was armed with a 32 pound cannon and a 12 pound brass Dahlgren pivot gun but only eight rounds of 32 pound ammunition were found, a supply so small it was impossible to repel the trio of steamers bearing down upon him. A frantic search of the captured vessel failed to disclose any more rounds for the cannon and none for the pivot gun. Unknown to him, some ninety rounds of 32 pound ammunition were indeed stored in the cutter, never to be discovered by the Confederates.

Read had been so efficient in attaining the objects of his cruise that it is difficult to explain his failure to prepare for action. Common sense should have told him that United States Revenue cutters in wartime would have to carry more ammunition than he found, and he certainly had the time to look. Anyone with even a moderate amount of sailing experience can testify that the one commodity in abundance during a passage in extremely light air is time, which hangs like a shroud over the entire crew. Had Read used the eight hour's grace he had been given to prepare for action, the result might well have been different for his pursuers were not warship-built and designed to take punishment; they were merchant vessels overloaded with men.

The only reasonable explanation would seem to be fatigue. The crew of first *Florida*, then *Tacony*, then *Archer*, and now *Cushing* must have been exhausted when they boarded their prize. It had been a grueling seven weeks, punctuated by three transfers, climaxed by a midnight raid and crowned with a back-breaking night at the oars towing the heavy cutter. The probability is that, under these circumstances, Read and men simply forgot to put their house in order. At any rate, knowing it was to cost them their freedom they determined to sell themselves as dearly as possible.

When the pursuing pack of steamers was within two miles of *Cushing*, the Confederates opened fire, sending all eight shots at *Forest City*. Their aim was not bad for an exhausted crew at a strange gun, but it was not quite good enough, the last shot falling within thirty feet of the steamer. The next few shots would certainly have disposed of *Forest City*, but, unknown to Read, they were reposing undiscovered below decks in *Cushing*. The officer in charge of the artillery aboard *Forest City*, First Lieutenant Edward Collins of the Seventeenth Infantry, did not return the fire since he had but one 6 pounder field piece and one 12 pounder howitzer, and he was reserving them for boarding.

With neither the wind to move his prize nor the means to defend her, Read determined that, if he could not have her, neither should the Yankees; accordingly he determined to destroy her. He notified Davenport that the vessel was to be sunk and assigned one of the cutter's boats for him and his crew. Twenty men and boys of the original crew got into the boat still handcuffed, but, at the request of the crew, the keys to the handcuffs were thrown into the boat, the cuffs were then unlocked and the liberated captives pulled away from the schooner.

The Confederates then set fire to *Cushing*, and manning the remaining two boats were promptly made prisoners by *Forest City*, the original crew of the cutter being picked up by *Chesapeake*. Some time between noon and two p.m. *Cushing* blew up, and the little flotilla returned to Portland where they took possession of *Archer* which, having been left by the Confederates with a crew of three, was attempting to escape. With her they recovered *Tacony*'s log book, flag and her prizes, together with six chronometers from that vessel and her prizes, all but one of which were still functioning.

This ended the *Tacony* affair. The chartered vessels went back to their normal duties and disappeared into history, all except *Chesapeake*. Six months later she was hijacked while on her regular run from New York to Portland, taken to Nova Scotia, and became the object of a dispute between the United States and Great Britain.

For the size of his crew and the short length of his voyage, Read had achieved considerable success. At the very minimum, he got the attention not only of the Navy Department but of the Union merchant marine and insurance industries, and he disrupted affairs on the Eastern seaboard to a degree disproportionate to his resources. By any standard, he had carried out his orders and done so without attaining any of the odium which characterized other raiders in later, more modern and presumably more civilized wars.

* * *

The entire affair will be found in O.R.N. I, Volume 2, in two locations. The first runs from page 273 to page 349 and contains the majority of the material used herein. Maffitt's and Read's reports are at pp. 644 and 655.

CHAPTER XIV

The *Chesapeake* Affair

Perhaps the Confederate Navy's most spectacular successes were obtained by its commerce raiders, *Alabama* and *Florida,* commanded by officers in the regular navy, but there were other commerce raiders whose status, while legal, was irregular. These were the privateers and vessels with letters of marque. Without going into technicalities, both of these were, in effect, licenses issued by the Confederate government to private individuals authorizing them to raid Union commerce. This had been the time honored method in which America had made war against Britain in the War of 1812. However, the method had fallen into disfavor; an international treaty (which the United States refused to sign) outlawed it, and the Union never employed it. The Confederacy, which stood in relation to the Union in much the same way the United States had stood in relation to Britain in 1812, nevertheless engaged in the practice and turned privateers and letters of marque loose on the North.

International law strictly construed these letters against the privateers for it is obvious that the practice is only one step removed from piracy. One of these letters of marque irregularly produced an "auxiliary unit" which went on a diversion of its own and became the object of a chase which threatened to intensify the smoldering dispute with Great Britain over the rights of a belligerent and which came to be known as "The Chesapeake Affair."*

*   *   *

If Captain Isaac Willett congratulated himself on his good fortune when he retired to his cabin on the night of 6 December 1863, he could surely be forgiven. As master of the steamship *Chesapeake*, trading regularly between New York City and Portland, Maine, he had gained national notoriety when he had successfully pursued the stolen revenue cutter *Caleb Cushing* six months earlier. He had a good ship, a good cargo and a payload of passengers. He and *Chesapeake* were then some twenty miles east of Cape Cod, about half way to Portland. All was right with the world, or so he thought.

Between midnight and one a.m. on the 7th that world collapsed on Captain Willett. Chief Mate Charles Johnson awakened him with the news that his second engineer had been shot. Willett, leaving his cabin to investigate, was himself shot at four times. When he entered the pilot house "First Lieutenant" Henry A. Parr collared him, taking him a prisoner on his own ship "in the name of the Southern Confederacy." *Chesapeake* had been stolen.

The events leading up to this predicament had originated several months earlier. On 27 October 1862, the Confederate government issued a letter of marque to Thomas B. Power, captain of the schooner *Retribution*. For reasons not clear, Power transferred his command to "John Parker," that being the alias of Vernon G. Locke, an Englishman. After cruising for a while, the unseaworthy *Retribution* was taken to Nassau in the Bahamas, where she was

---

* Actually, this was the navy's second *Chesapeake* affair. On June 22, 1807, HMS *Leopard* had brutalized the unprepared and poorly handled USS *Chesapeake*, one of the original ships of the United States Navy, and had pressed members of her crew into British service. Nevertheless, the 1863 event has gone into the Official Records as "The *Chesapeake* Affair," ORN I, 2, 512 &c. and is treated here as such.

condemned and sold, thus depriving Parker of his command. Parker and two subordinates, Parr and John C. Braine, then went to St. John, New Brunswick, where they contrived the scheme of capturing *Chesapeake*. Parker "commissioned" Braine and Parr to proceed to New York with what men they could get, take passage on *Chesapeake* or any Federal steamer, and capture her as opportunity should offer. No official connection between the Confederate government and the so-called "commissioning" of Braine and Parr existed except the tenuous thread of the letter of marque through Power.[1]

Braine and Parr did exactly what they had been ordered to do. They, together with fifteen others, booked passage on *Chesapeake* from New York to Portland, went aboard, and bided their time. Off Cape Cod they seized their chance and made a violent capture, subduing Captain Willett, killing the second engineer, Owen Schaffer, wounding the chief mate in the right knee and left arm, and shooting the chief engineer, James Johnson, in the hollow of his chin. Parr then placed Willett in handcuffs and confiscated the ship's papers.

Conspirator Robert Osbourn navigated *Chesapeake* north past Mount Desert, Maine, to Seal Cove Harbor on Grand Manan, a few miles off the coast of Maine, where, for some unexplained reason, three or four men went ashore for a short time. After their return *Chesapeake* steamed up the Bay of Fundy to St. John, the principal port of the province of New Brunswick.

At St. John, Parker took command, allowing the passengers and crew including Willett to go ashore. The Confederates kept Willett's firearms but permitted him to take his clock (most likely a chronometer), eight charts, his sextant and three books. Apparently the conspirators had come prepared with their own navigational equipment, since a sextant and an accurate chronometer were absolutely necessary for offshore navigation and charts were needed for coastwise piloting. The Confederates also detained two engineers and three firemen to work the engine room.

The conspirators had intended to run directly to Wilmington, North Carolina, but *Chesapeake* did not carry enough coal for that voyage, so they headed instead for Shelbourne, Nova Scotia, and thence to several other small Nova Scotian ports, winding up at Sambro, a small harbor just west of Halifax, where they were successful in securing coal. By this time Willett had broken the story, however, and the United States Navy was in full pursuit.

On 9 December, two days after the takeover, Commodore Hiram Paulding, commandant of the Brooklyn Navy Yard, tele-graphed Secretary of the Navy Gideon Welles of the capture. Five minutes later a similar telegram from Governor John Andrew of Massachusetts arrived. Welles was surprised by neither, however, since H.B. Cromwell & Co of New York had already telegraphed him offering two steamers, free of cost, for pursuit. A flurry of other similar telegrams made for a busy afternoon for Mr. Secretary Welles who promptly ordered a general chase to begin at the earliest moment. In compliance, USS *Acacia, Ella and Annie, Agawam, Dacotah, Ticonderoga, Niagara, Sebago, Grand Gulf* and *Vicksburg* sailed promptly for the chase (*Agawam* departing so hastily that she left her commanding officer behind). Only *Ella and Annie, Dacotah* and *Niagara* were to play any significant part in the chase.

Ella and Annie, built just before the war for the southern trade, had been a blockade runner but was captured by USS *Niphon* on 9 November 1863 and taken to Boston for condemnation. She was refitting at the Boston Navy Yard when the *Chesapeake* hijacking took place. Her very brief deck log does not record that she was ever formally placed in commission but that she received a crew at 10:40 a.m. 18 December and got under way at 1:40 p.m. under the temporary command of Acting Volunteer Lieutenant J. Frederick Nickels.*

---

* Her deck log, which is in the National Archives, must be one of the shortest on record. It commences with the reception of her crew on 10 December 1863, the roster of which does not appear, and ends with her return to Boston before the end of the month. On 9 February 1864 she was formally commissioned as USS *Malvern* and under that name became famous as the flagship of Rear Admiral David D. Porter, commander of the North Atlantic Blockading Squadron.

After searching several Nova Scotian harbors, *Ella and Annie* arrived at Halifax during the afternoon of 15 December. Following up rumors, she then called at Le Have, Lunenberg, and then at Sambro Harbor where on 17 December she discovered a steamer lying at anchor with a schooner alongside coaling her. At her appearance, some unknown person aboard the steamer quickly hoisted the American flag upside down, the generally recognized call of distress. *Chesapeake* had been apprehended securely anchored in a British port.

Nickels wasted little time. He drove *Ella and Annie* alongside *Chesapeake* and boarded her but found that all the "pirates" except two had departed. The coaling operation, which had ceased when *Ella and Annie* appeared, was resumed. The schooner was searched, turning up trunks and packages taken from *Chesapeake*, and another Confederate was found concealed under buffalo robes as the previous two found on *Chesapeake* had been. Putting the three prisoners in double irons, Nickels completed coaling and got under way for the United States in company with *Chesapeake*. Just outside the harbor he encountered USS *Dacotah*, a 227 foot screw sloop under the command of Commander Albert G. Clary. *Dacotah* was not surprised: "At 11:20 [a.m.] discovered a lead colored steamer in the care of a black steamer. [The lead colored] Steamer proved to be the U.S. Gun Boat *Ella and Annie* and the captured steamer *Chesapeake* which had been recaptured by the *Ella and Annie* together with three of her crew."[2]

Clary, the senior officer and thus in tactical command, recognized at once the seriousness of the situation. Great Britain had actually begun to transfer troops to Canada in preparation for war with the United States after Commodore Charles Wilkes aboard *San Jacinto* had violated neutrality by taking Confederate envoys from the decks of the Royal Mail Steamer *Trent* back in 1861. And that had been on the high seas, whereas *Chesapeake* had been snatched from the security of a neutral British port and was being taken to a port of the capturing belligerent power.

In a masterpiece of tactful understatement, Clary reported, "In an interview with this officer [Nickels] advised him to proceed at once to Halifax, that steps might be taken to legalize the capture."[3] Nickels put it a little more bluntly: "[I] fell in with the U.S. sloop of war *Dacotah*, Captain Clary, who hailed us and asked if that was the *Chesapeake*. I replied in the affirmative. He then asked 'Where do you proceed with your prize?' I replied, 'To Boston.' He then asked, 'Did you catch the pirates?' I replied I had but three. He then told me to repair on board. I went on board, where he ordered me to proceed to Halifax with the prize for adjudication, at which place we arrived and dropped anchor at 3:45 p.m."[4]

Clary's actions, without a doubt, saved the United States from further humiliation. When Secretary of the Navy Welles learned of Nickels' understandable desire to bring *Chesapeake* to a Northern port and before he was apprised of Clary's actions, he was so disturbed that he kept the messenger who had brought the news waiting while he drafted hasty orders to return *Chesapeake* to Canada forthwith.[5]

Halifax has enjoyed a checkered relationship with the United States and its navy. It was a friend and protector in the halcyon days before the American Revolution when employed by the British as a base of operations against the French fortress of Louisbourg during the French and Indian Wars. During the American Revolution, it had received as settlers large numbers of Loyalists, who had been expelled from their homes in the rebelling colonies. In that war and the War of 1812, it was a base of operations for the British Navy against the Americans. It was to Halifax that HMS *Shannon* escorted USS *Chesapeake* after defeating her off Boston Light in the War of 1812.* In the First and Second World Wars it was a base for American warships. It was to

---

* This was the same frigate which had been so humiliated by HMS *Leopard*. No fighting ship of the United States Navy has ever borne the name *Chesapeake* since that day.

Halifax that *American* warships now escorted another captured *Chesapeake*.

Clary immediately communicated with the U.S. consul and the provincial authorities and telegraphed a report to Secretary Welles. He directed his first lieutenant (executive officer) to wait upon the consul and, with the consul, to call upon the provincial secretary. The consul, who seems to have been in somewhat of a panic, delayed the official visit required by international protocol. By the time it was made the Canadians had learned of the three manacled prisoners aboard *Ella and Annie* and the Canadian provincial secretary, Charles Tupper, on the evening of the U.S. ships' arrival with their prize, wrote: "To the Officer in Command of the United States Ships of War at the Port of Halifax, Nova Scotia":

> Three war steamers bearing the flag of the United States having arrived here, and no officer belonging to either of them having reported himself to the administrator of the government or the officer in command of the troops in the garrison, I have it in command from his honor the administrator of the government to enquire the names of the ships under your command, the object of your visit to this port, and the circumstances under which the steamship *Chesapeake* has been this day taken out of the harbor of Sambro, a Nova Scotian port, and brought into this harbor by men-of-war belonging to the Navy of the United States.[6]

That same evening Clary put forth the olive branch. He replied to Tupper's curt inquiry, justifying his visit to Halifax as an inquiry whether the British authorities would receive *Chesapeake* or whether she should be taken to the United States for adjudication. Needless to say, the British opted to retain *Chesapeake*. The following morning Clary was advised of this decision and, further, that neither he nor "any vessel in the service of the U.S. Government" would be allowed to leave until the matter of the prisoners was settled.

Probably to Clary's great relief, in the early afternoon of the 19th a third American warship, the screw frigate *Niagara*, the largest

Confederate Secretary of State Judah Benjamin, a renowned attorney before and after the Civil War, personally oversaw many of the international legal disputes arising out of North-South naval engagements.

vessel in the Federal Navy, arrived under the command of Commodore Thomas T. Craven. Craven, although ill, relieved Clary of his diplomatic responsibilities and conducted all further negotiations with the British. He found himself in the position of a poker player with poor cards whose opponent has just doubled his bet. He acted as a good poker player would: he folded.

Realizing that the three prisoners would have to be given up, he went to the American consulate where he encountered Major General Hastings, the provincial governor, and obtained from him an agreement that the three prisoners would be arrested. Not surprisingly, the prisoners were allowed bail, which they immediately jumped. Apologies had been tendered, *Chesapeake* surrendered to the authorities, and the prisoners arrested. The American warships were permitted to depart, leaving the question of the custody of *Chesapeake* to the British courts to determine. This they did with all the deliberate procedure of their complex legal system. *Chesapeake* was held at Halifax until the middle of February.

The Confederate government was as embarrassed as the Federal government had been. Although it wanted *Chesapeake*, Secretary of State Judah P. Benjamin was astute enough to realize that its right to possession was extremely weak. Benjamin, who was one the keenest lawyers in North America,* recognized at once that Power's authority to transfer the letter of marque, issued to a ship and not to an individual, and Parker's right to "commission" an officer in the Confederacy were the decisive issues. He sent to Nova Scotia J. P. Holcombe, a prominent lawyer, as a special commissioner, with instructions to endeavor to obtain *Chesapeake* for the Confederacy despite the legal problems they both foresaw.

Benjamin's doubts were resolved on 15 February 1864 when Hon. Alexander Stewart, judge of the vice-admiralty court rendered a lengthy opinion, returned *Chesapeake* to her owners. In it he called the seizing of the vessel "a piratical taking," to the great discomfort of the Confederates, one of whom complained, "I do not believe any judicial proceeding has taken place in a British court for a century and a half so discreditable to its dignity, its intelligence, or its justice," No matter, *Chesapeake* immediately left Halifax and her place in history behind and resumed her normal routine.

---

* After the defeat of the Confederacy he escaped to England where he was admitted to the English bar and thereafter wrote a textbook on the law of sales which remained a classic in both England and America until comparatively modern times.

CHAPTER XV

The Death of the *Louisiana*

The port of Wilmington, North Carolina, some twenty miles up the Cape Fear River had been a thorn in the side of the Union since the Civil War began. Its proximity to Virginia and the Confederate armies there made it comparatively easy to quickly forward smuggled arms and ammunition to the troops. Blockading the mouth of the Cape Fear presented a difficult problem to the navy because there were two entrances separated by such extensive sand bars that the navigational distance between them was about fifty miles. Strategically located between the two mouths and guarding both was Fort Fisher.

Fort Fisher, the principal defense of the entrance to the Cape Fear River and thus to the port of Wilmington, North Carolina, was situated facing the sea but on the east bank of the river on a sandy peninsula some twenty miles south of the port. Fort Fisher was not a massive masonry structure, such as Sumter or Morgan, but was composed primarily of huge sand dunes masking cannon aimed out to sea or sweeping the beach. Today the remains not swept away by the sea have been restored and are maintained by the State of North Carolina as a state park.

Artillery and naval gunfire were of little use against the fort: enemy projectiles buried themselves in soft

sand rather than shattering bricks and mortar. However, some fertile brain conceived the idea of blowing
it up: a ship loaded with gunpowder would be run
ashore as close to the fort as possible and blown up.
For this purpose USS *Louisiana* was chosen.

USS *Louisiana* was an iron, propeller driven vessel of 438 tons.
One hundred forty-three feet long, built in 1860, and acquired by
the Navy 10 July 1861, she served continuously in the Carolina
sounds until ten minutes before two in the morning of 24 December 1864, when, in an attempt to destroy Fort Fisher, North
Carolina, she was done in by her own people. Her end was
ineffective and the final irony is that it was unnecessary.

The Official Records tell one story of *Louisiana*'s death; Rear
Admiral David D. Porter tells another. The difference between
them is enlightening. From what appears in the records, it is
inferable that the idea originated with Assistant Secretary of the
Navy Gustavus V. Fox. Certainly, Fox was in on the plan from the
beginning.

On 27 November 1864 he forwarded to Porter, then commander of the North Atlantic Blockading Squadron at Hampton
Roads, Virginia, documents detailing reports and studies by Chief
Engineer of the Army Richard Delafield, Major J.M. Benton,
commander of the Washington Arsenal, and Lieutenant Commander William N. Jeffers, of the Washington Navy Yard, together
with the minutes of a meeting held 23 November, all concerning
the proposed exploding of a vessel near enough to Fort Fisher to
stun the garrison and make the capture of the fort feasible. Only
Major Benton's report was favorable and even his was diluted: "The
little attention and thought which I have been able to give this
subject, and the absence of all practical experience in the effect of
such explosions, will, I fear, make my opinion of little practical
value."[1] Nevertheless, the ad hoc committee determined to go
ahead with the project, estimating during its deliberations that the

nearest safe distance from the doomed vessel would be five miles.[2] Fox then sent the papers to Admiral Porter for his opinion.

David D. Porter[3] was a man of both ideas and action: he rose from commander to rear admiral during the war and became the Navy's second full admiral thereafter. Examples of his enthusiasm, his courage and his ability to manage both ships and men fill the Official Records but his post war contributions, including the founding of the United States Naval Institute, quite possibly exceed his wartime contributions. It is hard to tell whether Porter's flamboyance and impetuosity or his great intelligence and decisive action dominated, but he was invariably involved in action of one sort or another.

Writing twenty years after the war,[4] Porter related in dramatic and humorous detail how Major General Benjamin F. Butler, the area commander, and his chief of staff came on board his flagship *Malvern*, accompanied by a shorthand reporter, and, with an air of great secrecy, advised him that he had an important communication. Porter derided the idea:

> I had not the faintest idea what he was driving at. It certainly could not be a balloon attack, for we had no balloons, and couldn't get them without an act of Congress. Perhaps, thought I, he intends to introduce rattlesnakes into Fort Fisher on the sly; but this idea I at once dismissed; there was nothing in the Constitution which would authorize such a proceeding.
>
> I whispered to Captain [K. Randolph] Breese, The general is going to propose his "petroleum bath," such as he has proposed to use on the James River. He is going to attack Fort Fisher from seaward by setting afloat tons of petroleum when the wind is on shore, and, by igniting it, knock the rebs out of their boots! I thought the absurdity of such an idea would be a great recommendation, especially as it would cost a great deal of money, for at that time there was a great competition in Washington as to which department could make the largest expenditure.
>
> After General Butler and his staff had departed, Captain Breese said to me: "Admiral, you certainly don't believe in that idea of a

powder-boat. It has about as much chance of blowing up the fort as I have of flying!"

And who knows, I said, whether a machine may not soon be perfected to enable us all to fly, as it only requires a forty-horse power in a cubic foot of space, and a propeller that will make such a vacuum that the air will rush in and drive the thing along.

Breese sighed as he walked out of the cabin, and I thought I heard him say "All bosh!"—but one has to be a little deaf occasionally."[5]

Porter concealed these sentiments admirably. On 8 December he directed Lieutenant Commander Pendleton G. Watmough to find the ideal spot for running the powder vessel ashore. He then selected *Louisiana* as the vessel to be destroyed, and chose as her commanding officer Commander Alexander C. Rhind, captain of the gunboat *Agawam* giving him the following flamboyant order:

"SIR: You will proceed, when ready, with the *Louisiana*, under your command...and place the vessel as close to Fort Fisher as the water will permit, even to running her on the beach. When she is there she is to be exploded...at such time as in your judgment may seem best.

"I have furnished you with all the means at my disposal...to make this thing successful and, if successful the credit will be yours. Great risks have to be run and there are chances that you may lose your life in this adventure; but the risk is worth the running, when the importance of the object is to be considered and the fame to be gained by this novel undertaking."

Perhaps to encourage poor Rhind, Porter then waxed poetic:

"I do not anticipate such a dreadful earthquake as some suppose will take place (destroying everything), nor do I think the effect will in any way be mild.

"I take a mean between the two, and think the explosion will be simply very severe, stunning men at a distance of three or four

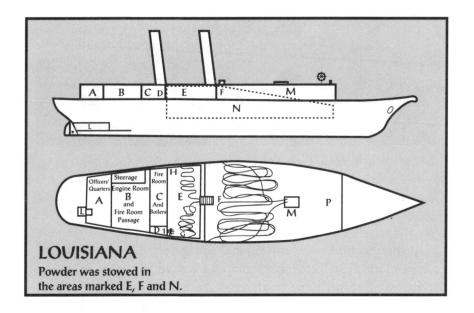

LOUISIANA
Powder was stowed in
the areas marked E, F and N.

hundred yards, demoralizing them completely, and making them
unable to stand for any length of time a fire from the ships.

"I think that houses in Wilmington and Smithville will tumble
to the ground and much demoralize the people, and I think if the
rebels fight after the explosion they have much more in them than
I gave them credit for.[6]

Rhind, with a volunteer crew from *Agawam*, set about his
business. Receiving *Louisiana* at Craney Island, adjacent to the
Norfolk Navy Yard, he filled her forward parts with 215 tons of
powder, all stowed forward since the engines occupied the after
part. On 18 December *Louisiana* left Beaufort, North Carolina,
in company with the tug *Wilderness*. After some debate over the
proper manner of affixing fuses, the weather, and coordination
with the army forces, Rhind ran *Louisiana* aground 250 yards from
Fort Fisher and seventy-five yards from shore. Rhind demonstrated
his courage and coolness when, after he had fired the fuses,
discovering that *Louisiana* was not holding her proper position, he
calmly stayed long enough to set another anchor before setting off
in the small boat which had been left for him.

Behind the Confederate earthworks at Fort Fisher. Such fortifications proved to be more capable of withstanding Union bombardment than stone fortresses.

In the meantime the entire blockading fleet had withdrawn to a minimum distance of five miles and waited. For a moment the scene was illuminated, then the darkness settled down, and all was still as before—no sound or movement in the fort indicating that any damage had been done. In fact, the Confederates took the explosion for that of a blockade runner with a quantity of ammunition on board, and were not all troubled about the matter.

Louisiana did not go gently into that good night—but she went without doing damage to anyone but herself. The other blockading vessels merely noted the blast and the time, while Colonel George Lamb, the fort commander noted in his official diary, "A blockader got aground near fort; set fire to herself and blew up."

The explosion had been planned to signal the start of an amphibious invasion by General Butler and his army troops. It petered out when Butler, after surveying the ground from a distance, decided the fort was impregnable, withdrew his troops and returned to Norfolk. This withdrawal triggered such a reaction that Butler was dismissed and replaced by Major General Alfred H. Terry, who returned in January with the same troops and, in conjunction with a naval bombardment and support from Porter and his fleet, assaulted and captured the fort, closing the Confederacy's last port.

Despite his dismissal, Butler retained a great deal of political influence and in January 1865 appeared before the Committee on the Conduct of the War, a congressional committee that was unfriendly to the Lincoln administration. His hardly unbiased testimony was highly critical of the navy and Rhind, who had survived the event without injury, felt himself aggrieved by Butler's testimony. In November 1865, he forwarded a rebuttal to the Secretary of the Navy, Gideon Welles:

> Had I been made aware that the proposition to employ the powder vessel as a preliminary to the attack on Fort Fisher was originated by General Butler, or that he expected such remarkable results from it, I should have required, as a condition on undertaking so hazardous a service (unsought by me) that General Butler or one of his then numerous attachs should have accompanied the party.

Quoting testimony from the record he became sarcastic in response to a question on the distance between the powder vessel and the fort: "Answer by General B. F. Butler, he being at the time of the explosion at or near Beaufort, (distance 60 to 70 miles)...I regret that the committee did not do me justice to summon me to reply to the evidence of General Butler."[7] Porter, after declaring that he had determined to do everything he could to make the experiment a success "even though he knew it was all folly," declared,

> When, after the lapse of twenty years, we think of this futile attempt to destroy so powerful a work as Fort Fisher, at the risk of so many valuable lives, in order that the pet scheme of a Major-General of Volunteers should be carried out, we may wonder that any one should countenance such an absurdity. The only powder needed was that fired from the cannon of the ships and what would have been fired from the muskets of the gallant soldiers had they been permitted by their commanding general to advance on the enemy."[8]

Although there are obviously two schools of thought on this matter, visiting Fort Fisher today and standing on the huge

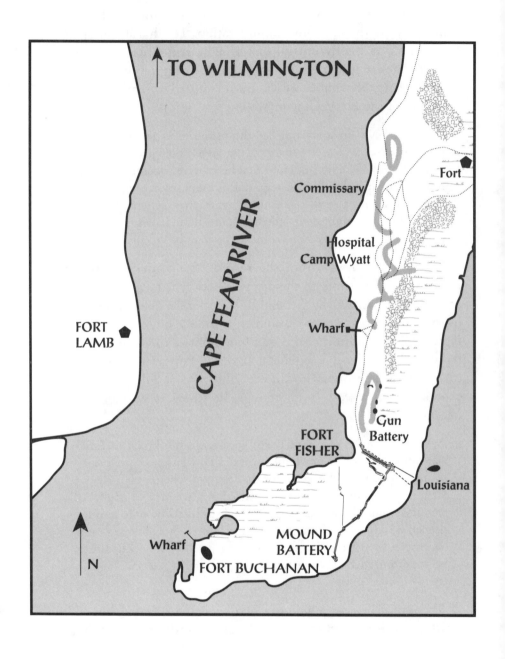

TO WILMINGTON

CAPE FEAR RIVER

Commissary

Fort

Hospital
Camp Wyatt

FORT
LAMB

Wharf

Gun
Battery

FORT
FISHER

Louisiana

N

Wharf

MOUND
BATTERY

FORT BUCHANAN

Better known for his later role in the Indian wars, Major General Alfred H. Terry succeeded where all others had failed by finally capturing Fort Fisher for the Union.

mounds of sand behind which the Confederates were entrenched, it is difficult to understand how the explosion could have seriously affected the men protected by them. This does not, however, in any way detract from the heroism of Rhind and his crew who succeeded in a mission assigned to them by a commander who had put it in writing that they probably would not survive.

As for the murdered *Louisiana*, Porter added, "Had she not gone up in a blaze of glory she might to-day have figured on the navy-list as an effective vessel of war, while slowly decaying at her berth in Rotten Row!" One would like to think that *Louisiana*, given the choice, would have preferred to go the way she did.

CHAPTER XVI

To Fight or Not to Fight?—The Dilemma of Commodore Craven

Clearly it is a professional naval officer's duty to engage the enemy whenever possible. While rules of engagement may vary, all navies require that in time of war a commander must engage an enemy so long as it is in his power to do so, unless good reasons to the contrary exist. The question of what constitutes good and sufficient reasons may require much soul searching on the part of a commander. Those whose decision proves correct become household names; those who fail court disaster. Commodore Thomas T. Craven was one of those required to make such a decision.

*   *   *

Commodore Thomas T. Craven[1] had demonstrated since the early days of the war that he was no coward. He had commanded *Brooklyn* under then Flag Officer David G. Farragut at the passage of Forts St. Philip and Jackson in 1862, giving and receiving as much fire as any one present. He had then taken *Brooklyn* up the river to Vicksburg and participated in the fighting there. Unfortunately, after a dispute with Farragut, he received a letter of such reprimand from that doughty admiral that he lost his good judgment and requested a transfer, writing angrily, "You were pleased to address such a letter to me as no officer possessing the least particle of self respect could receive submissively without degrad-

The armored ram CSS Stonewall, *the most advanced ship of its type then afloat.*

ing himself to the level of a serf."² This error of judgment had cost him his command.

In March 1865, during the closing days of the war, Craven was in command of the steam frigate *Niagara* searching for Confederate commerce raiders and cruising in company with USS *Sacramento* off the coasts of Spain and Portugal, when he found CSS *Stonewall* lying in the harbor of Ferrol, Spain. He promptly took *Niagara* and *Sacramento* into Corunna, a port a few miles away from which he could watch the Confederate ironclad.

Stonewall was the last, but by no means the least, of all the Confederate rams. Some 170 feet long, covered with five and a half inches of iron, and armed with one 300 and two 250 pound Armstrong rifles and with a speed of 13 knots, she represented the state of the art in that type of vessel.

Against her were pitted *Niagara,* a wooden vessel of approximately equal speed, and *Sacramento*, likewise wooden, with a speed of 12.5 knots and armed with but three 100 pound Parrott rifles and six 8 inch smooth bores. Despite the ships' difference in construction, the odds against the Federals were not as heavy as might be imagined. *Niagara*, 345 feet long, had been the largest vessel ever built in the United States when she was commissioned in 1857, and she was armed with twelve 9 inch smoothbores rifled, eleven 11 inch smooth bore guns and one 80 pound rifle.

Although the war had clearly been won by March 1865, the Union Navy feared that *Stonewall* might break loose and cause great damage, either to the Union commerce, the coastal cities of the North, or to both. Correspondence in the Official Records reflects as much panic over *Stonewall* as there ever was over *Virginia* before she was checkmated by *Monitor*. Because of this, *Niagara* and *Sacramento* kept a close eye on *Stonewall*, hoping to prevent her escaping from the port. On 21 March and again on the 23rd, having prepared for action by stripping the ship of rigging down to her lower masts, *Stonewall* left her anchorage and stood out some two miles from the entrance to the harbor to force a confrontation but, in Craven's words, "the state of the sea was not favorable for her purposes" and when the Federal ships sortied out of Corunna to meet her, she retreated to her old berth. On the 24th the face-off reoccurred. Craven did not accept the challenge:

> [A] dead calm prevailing, with a smooth, glassy sea, she again made her appearance. At this time the odds in her favor were too great and too certain, in my humble judgment, to admit of the slightest hope of being able to inflict upon her even the most trifling injury, whereas, if we had gone out, the *Niagara* would most undoubtedly have been easily and promptly destroyed. So thoroughly a one-sided combat I did not consider myself called upon to engage in.[3]

Craven was not the only one to consider *Stonewall* a formidable adversary. Walke, the captain of *Sacramento*, himself no stranger to the enemy's fire, felt the same way for he reported: "Her turrets

The formidable ram of the CSS Stonewall. *It could probably have sunk both of Commodore Craven's wooden ships without using its Armstrong guns.*

are of the heaviest plating and, as reported by Mr. Palmer (an American and now a chief engineer in the Spanish navy)...she is shot proof from any quarter."[4]

Early the next morning *Stonewall* got under way and, eluding the blockading Federals, arrived at Lisbon on 26 March. Craven followed her, arriving on the 27th, when he committed the tactical error of entering port with both of his vessels, thus subjecting them to the twenty-four hour rule. This rule of international law required that warships of opposing powers lying in a neutral port must not depart within twenty-four hours of each other. It was (and still is) strictly enforced by neutral powers and because of it Craven had painted himself into a corner.

On the 28th, *Stonewall* sailed. When Craven attempted to follow her he was fired on by the Spanish forts, had to break off the pursuit and return to his anchorage and lost her for good:

After forty-five days of constant watchfulness, at times buoyed up with the hope that she might be detained definitively at Ferrol....I have now been compelled to lose sight of one of the most formidable ironclad vessels now afloat. It may appear to some that I ought to have run the hazard of a battle, but according to my judgment I shall ever feel that I have done all that could properly be attempted toward retarding the operations and progress of that vessel.[5]

Craven put it more glumly in a letter to the chargè d'affaires at Madrid:

With feelings that no one can appreciate, I was obliged to undergo the deep humiliation of knowing that she...was there, steaming back and forth, flaunting her flags, and waiting for me to go out to the attack. *I dared not do it!* The condition of the sea was such that it would have been perfect madness for me to go out. We could not possibly have inflicted the slightest injury upon her; and should have exposed ourselves to almost instant destruction—a one-sided combat which I do not consider myself called upon to engage in.

Craven's explanation of his failure to pursue *Stonewall* is unclear and led to his court martial. Three-quarters of a century later a British commodore faced a similar situation when he encountered the German pocket battleship *Graf Spee*. He ran the risk, defeated *Graf Spee*, and became an admiral.

By the time this news had been digested at the Navy Department, the war was over, Abraham Lincoln was dead, and *Stonewall*, which had sailed to Cuba only to be interned was turned over to the United States, no longer a menace to the Union cause. Nevertheless, Commodore Craven was ordered tried by court martial.

Craven's report undoubtedly arrived at the Navy Department during the period of confusion and turmoil which accompanied the end of the war and the almost simultaneous assassination of Lincoln. Gideon Welles makes no mention of the affair even though he had been keeping his eye on *Stonewall*—and Craven:

March 20, Monday. Seward sent me a half-scary letter from Sanford, who is in Paris, that Page [commanding *Stonewall*] intends coming out of Ferrol and fighting the *Niagara*...Craven is a good officer, though a little timid and inert by nature. The occasion is a great one for him and will rouse his energies. I wish he had smooth bores instead of rifles on his vessel, provided they have a conflict; wish he was more of a rifle himself.

March 27, Monday. Had dispatches on Saturday from Craven, who is on the *Niagara* watching the rebel ironclad *Stonewall* at Corunna. He says he is "in an embarrassing and unenviable position." There are many of our best naval officers who think he has an enviable position, and they would make sacrifices to obtain it. Perhaps Craven will fight well, though his language is not bold and defiant, nor his sentiments such as will stimulate his crew. It is an infirmity. Craven is intelligent, and disciplines his ship well, I am told, but his constant doubts and misgivings impair his usefulness.[6]

Welles' diary records little other than details of the assassination and consequent change of government, until well after the time when reports of *Stonewall*'s escape must have reached him. We can fathom his reactions, however, since he ordered Craven tried on the charge of "failing to do his utmost to overtake and capture or destroy a vessel which it was his duty to encounter." The charge postulated that it was Craven's "duty to encounter" the Confederate, the specification reciting that Craven "did fail to use any exertions or make any effort whatever to overtake and capture or destroy the said vessel of the enemy as it was his duty to have done."

The court convened at Washington on 7 November 1865 and, remembering their earlier differences, Craven may have been dismayed to see his old commander, Farragut, acting as president. Indeed, the court seemed a Civil War naval hall of fame, including Admirals Hiram Paulding, who had tried to prevent the loss of the Norfolk Navy Yard in 1861; Charles H. Davis who had fought alongside Farragut and Craven at Vicksburg; John A. Dahlgren who had commanded at Charleston, Commodore John A. Winslow who had sunk *Alabama*, and Captain (formerly Acting

Commodore Craven's ship, USS Niagara, *at Antwerp. Union naval vessels patrolled European ports throughout the Civil War, looking for Confederate raiders.*

Rear Admiral) S. Phillips Lee who had commanded the North Atlantic Blockading Squadron.

This court of distinguished combat veterans rendered a compromise verdict and like all compromise verdicts, this one contained inconsistencies. The court stated, "Specification of the charge proven, except in so far as the words 'as it was his duty to have done' declare it to have been the imperative duty of the accused to join battle." It added that it did not wish to deprive an officer of the discretionary power due to his command nor to establish the principle that it is "always and under all circumstances imperative that two wooden vessels should attack an ironclad." It did censure Craven for not keeping *Stonewall* under constant observation and for remaining at anchor while his enemy was active. The court imposed the astounding sentence of suspension from duty on leave pay for a period of two years!

To say that Secretary Welles disapproved of the proceedings would be an understatement. On 1 December he sent the record right back to the court "for a revision of the finding, which...is in conflict with the law and...would tend to render the provisions of law...a 'dead letter.'" Faced with this rebuke, the court revised its verdict, finding Craven guilty "except the words 'as it was his duty to have done.'"

Upon the revised verdict, which mirrored the first one, the court imposed the same penalty. This made Welles even angrier. On 6 December he issued a general order disapproving the findings of the court and castigating it for both its findings and its sentence:

> If it was the duty of the accused to encounter the *Stonewall* and, through negligence or any other fault, he failed in any one particular to do his duty, then he did not do his utmost...and is guilty of the charge preferred against him...Such is the necessary inference from what the court find proved...They say they find the specification of the charge proven except the words "as it was his duty to have done." This exception destroys and annihilates the gravamen of the charge... If...it is not proved that it was his duty to encounter the vessel, then he is not proved guilty of the charge...and the court have committed a grave error in finding him guilty.
>
> The court, in this case of conviction of a capital offense, has adjudged a punishment which is obviously nothing more than a nominal punishment, if it be even as much. Suspension from duty for two years on "leave pay" is in itself nothing more than leave of absence for the same period...Such punishment as this no officer could obtain from the Department as a favor.

He concluded his diatribe with the following caustic comment:

> [The] inference is that the general rule with a commanding officer of the Navy should be "Do not fight if there is a chance of defeat," rather than the converse rule, "Fight if there is a chance of victory." The principle uniformly inculcated as a rule of naval action has been that it is the first duty of a commander in war to take great risks for the accomplishment of great ends.

Commodore Thomas T. Craven, who faced a court martial for failing to engage the CSS Stonewall.

With that, Welles set aside the proceedings, relieved Craven from arrest, and restored him to duty. As he did so, he grumbled to himself in his diary, "A court martial of high officers in the case of Craven, who declined to encounter the *Stonewall*, has made itself ridiculous by an incongruous finding and award which I cannot approve. It is not pleasant to encounter so large a number of officers of high standing, but I must do my duty if they do not."[7]

Later, after the order of revocation was published, he maintained, "The proceedings were a shocking jumble, a fellow feeling probably among some members of the court. I should not be surprised if Farragut's kind and generous heart acquiesced against his better judgment, but I do not know."[8]

Twenty years after the war Admiral David D. Porter analyzed the verdict's inconsistency:[9]

It is a well-established principle in military or naval law, that when charges are brought against an officer to any one of which the penalty of death is attached, no other sentence can be awarded. The law is imperative that courts martial shall adjudge a punishment adequate to the offence committed and only leaves it discretionary with the court to *recommend* the convicted person to clemency, that clemency to be exercised only by the reviewing authority....In the case under consideration, the court may have deemed that the law under which the accused was tried was one of a harsh character, as, no doubt, it was, but it was bound by a solemn obligation to administer it as it stood on the statute books, and not to modify it to suit their own views of justice.

The great mistake the court made was in endeavoring to modify the charge of which the accused was or was not guilty....Three of the officers had some rough experiences with iron clad rams, and, under the circumstances, were no doubt willing to allow the commander of the *Niagara* discretionary rights in regards to attacking the *Stonewall.*

As this case ended, the matter is left in abeyance, and it may yet happen that an officer may be tried under the same circumstances which present the simple question: Shall an officer be allowed any discretionary power in deciding whether or not to do battle with an enemy's ships or with an enemy's forts.[10]

While Welles tried to explain away the verdict by blaming the "old boys" fraternity, he missed the point. Craven had certainly given Farragut no reason to go out of his way to help him; the other members of the court had done their share in the war and knew the rules at least as well, and probably better, than did Welles. What the case did was highlight a commander's dilemma when adverse odds are high and the stakes are small. It was clear by the end of that March that the war could end only one way, and that it was going to end very soon. The Confederacy lay in ruins; its armed forces were facing defeat and *Stonewall* could be, at worst, only a nuisance. To pit two wooden vessels against so formidable an adversary when there so little to gain would have been a wanton risk of lives when the war was already won.

It surely was difficult to explain to the families of those lost in *Congress* and *Cumberland* the reason for their bereavement at the hands of *Virginia*; it would have been equally, if not more, difficult to explain to newly bereaved families why wooden warships were unnecessarily pitted against iron when the war was so near a victorious conclusion. Possibly by returning the verdict for a second time, the court was gently reminding Welles he was wrong; enough blood had been shed, and it was now time to follow Lincoln's advice and bind up the nation's wounds. Despite the law, the court proved itself wiser than Welles, although there were better ways of showing it than by awarding the defendant a vacation with pay.

Chapter XVIII

Constitution's Last Race

When the United States Naval Academy was established in 1845, it was located in Annapolis, Maryland,
where it still remains on the site of old Fort Severn.
When the Civil War broke out in 1861, the proximity
of Annapolis to Washington, which at the outset was
almost under siege, led to fears that the Academy and
its attendant school ship, the frigate *Constitution*,
might be captured by the Confederates. Accordingly,
the academy and *Constitution* were transferred to Newport, Rhode Island, where they remained until the end
of the war, at which time they returned to Annapolis.
This trip down the coast was to provide *Constitution*
with her last hurrah.

*   *   *

Although she possessed the most distinguished record of any
American warship before or since, and had been the object of
veneration amounting almost to worship for several generations,
the simple truth was that, after sixty-four years of almost uninter-
rupted service, time had passed *Constitution* by. Obsolete in design, outmoded in power and equipment, and possessing no real
value either as a fighting ship or as a cruiser, her sole function was
to provide midshipmen with inspiration and knowledge.

Although some sailing vessels did take part in the war, their
services were generally employed where action was unlikely. After
Cumberland and *Congress* had been spectacularly destroyed by the

Confederate ironclad *Virginia*, formerly USS *Merrimack*, efforts were made to keep these wind-driven, wooden vessels away from such danger. Thus *Constellation*, the reconstructed near sister of *Constitution*, spent the better part of the war in the Mediterranean where both she and *St. Louis* were sent after the Confederate raiders *Sumter* and *Alabama*, wooden ships which they at least had some chance of besting. *Constitution*, probably because of her distinguished history and the sentimental attachment the country had for her, as well as her age, was relegated to a passive status. The very fact that she was now under the command of Lieutenant Commander Philip C. Johnson, Jr., instead of the four stripe captain she would have had in the old days was, in itself, a significant indication of her reduction in status.

Nobody seems to have entertained the thought of her getting to Annapolis by herself. When it had been decided that she was to accompany the academy from Annapolis to Newport (with orders to destroy her if capture seemed likely), she went at the end of a tow line. To those who remembered the vessel which had defeated the Tripolitans and later captured His Britannic Majesty's ships *Guerriere*, *Java*, *Cyane* and *Levant* (battering *Guerriere* and *Java* so heavily that they had to be destroyed after surrendering, lest they drown their own crews on their way to captivity) her passage down Chesapeake Bay, must have seemed to foretell the end, not only of an era but of the Union itself.

When the war was finished and the determination was made to return the Naval Academy and its attendant frigates to Annapolis, the question of how to get *Constitution* there was easy. She had come up under tow; she must return under the tow of the tug *Mercury*, with some assistance from her own sails if possible. Someone may just have entertained more ambitious ideas, however, for the preparations made for getting her under way smacked more of the departure on a foreign cruise than the transfer of an obsolete relic from one place to another.

It would not be possible for her to depart immediately for there was simply too much to be done to make her ready for sea.

216

*George Bancroft, foun-
der of the U.S. Naval
Academy.*

Although her masts and yards had been left standing, all the myriad lengths of running rigging, which enabled the sails to be raised, lowered and set at the proper angle to the wind, had been taken down and stored in the hold. They must now be brought out, examined, where necessary replaced, and finally restored to their proper position. This tedious process began on 27 June 1865 and took almost a month.

There was much more to do than simply getting the rigging in shape as the navy did not maintain its receiving ships or school ships in such condition as to enable them to put to sea immediately. Weather decks were roofed over so that they might be used in all climatic conditions. The great guns and their carriages were stowed elsewhere for safe keeping, enabling the gun deck to be converted into one huge open space. Partitions were then erected to divide this space into classrooms. In short, the vessel had become little more than a barn, a mere shell of the fighting ship she once had been. This process had to be reversed.

Nor was that the only task. Wooden ships are made of planks called strakes, fastened in some way or another to other timbers called frames. Since the strakes cannot be placed so closely together as to entirely prevent the entry of water, these spaces must be filled—from time to time; the process was not permanent—with cotton or other material by a process known as caulking. This never produces a totally waterproof ship, but it does make the entry of water manageable. Before *Constitution* could go to sea it was necessary to caulk not only her sides but her decks as well. This process began July 7 and continued almost down to the time she sailed.

Any object left immersed in sea water will inevitably acquire a growth of grass and barnacles, which will interfere with her speed unless removed by the laborious procedure of scraping it off manually, a tedious and tiresome process. Since *Constitution* had not had her bottom cleaned for several years, this was a necessary step before her departure. There being no dry dock in Newport, a diver was sent down on July 7 to scrape the bottom clean. To understate the case, this was not done in one day.

So completely had the aged vessel been stripped of her equipment that it was necessary to bring back aboard such navigational equipment as compasses and sextants. The great guns, which had been stored ashore, had to be brought back aboard and mounted, thus restoring her to at least the semblance of a fighting ship.

The final stage of preparation began on 31 July when the sails were bent on the masts. *Constitution* was designed to carry a full complement of thirty sails, making her an impressive sight to behold, as photographs and paintings of her demonstrate. However, inasmuch as it had been determined that her sails were only to be used to assist *Mercury* when possible, merely the foresail and mainsail, those great propulsion sails known as courses, were rigged to the fore and main masts, followed by the next higher tier, the topsails on all masts, fore, main and mizzen. The rest of those towering pillars of canvas which make all square-rigged ships, particularly *Constitution*, so impressive in appearance remained stowed below decks. In addition, provisions for the crew had to be stored away.

By 1 August the staging and partitions had been removed and all the educational material which would interfere with the operation of the vessel was dismounted. Two days later she commenced the process of disentangling herself from the pier, loading the last of the Naval Academy equipment to be transported, and taking on ammunition.

Loading ammunition in an antique vessel carrying outmoded guns immediately after the end of the greatest war in the nation's history may seem somewhat unnecessary, but there was good precedent. *Constitution's* half sister *Chesapeake* had been caught while disarmed, boarded and humiliated in peacetime by HMS *Leopard* back in 1807. Obviously there was no likelihood of such an affair in 1865 but, then, neither did there seem to be in 1807. The United States Navy had determined never to be caught like that again, particularly with a national monument! If she were to be attacked she would, at least, try to fight back.

The complicated process of restoration and making ready for sea was completed on 8 August. On that date *Constitution* received on board some forty-two women and children, families of men employed at the Naval Academy. Lacking specific details of where they were housed raises some interesting questions. There may have been some of the tiny cabins reserved for junior and warrant officers on the berth deck, but the chances are greater that a portion of one of the lower decks was set aside for their use. A reflection on that and the fact that the sanitary facilities were in the bows of the ship leads inexorably to the conclusion that the Victorians must not have been as modest as their descendants believe they were.

At 7:15 that evening the old warrior got underway at the end of a tow line from the designated tug, *Mercury*. This vessel was a twelve year old paddle wheel steamer, some 128 feet in length. The

Naval Academy class of 1866, some of the participants in Constitution's *last adventure.*

departure was purely symbolic; her log records that she anchored off Goat Island, bearing south by west, a distance of 250 yards. Any yachtsman familiar with Newport harbor realizes immediately that *Constitution* had hardly traveled a mile! The following morning, however, was the real commencement of what was probably the old warrior's most satisfactory, if not her most spectacular, run.

It began simply enough and probably not on time, for not until 11:15 did *Mercury* come alongside to take her tow line. She hardly did so in a seamanlike manner, running afoul of *Constitution's* bow, carrying away some of her gear and doing some minor damage, partly to the ship but probably more to her commander's disposition.

The incident proved more annoying than serious, however, and by 1:15 P. M. the *Constitution* and *Mercury* had passed Point Judith, fifteen miles southwest of Newport, and were headed south, southwest for the mouth of Chesapeake Bay. With the wind from the north, northwest at Force 3, (seven to ten miles per hour), and the convoy in the lee of the Connecticut and Long Island coast lines, the peaceful beginning must have given the dependent passengers hope for a pleasant, gentle voyage. Their wishes were to be at least partly fulfilled. *Constitution* and *Mercury* were making good all of three knots, about the speed of a plodding mule, and the weather was clear and mild.

This halcyon state of affairs continued the rest of that day, throughout the night and into the afternoon of the following day. Her position, according to her log, was determined to be Latitude 40°01'N, Longitude 72°W; the ships were well out into the Atlantic, and out of the protection of the mainland. In the forenoon watch the sails were set, probably to take some strain off the tow line, because the log records that *Mercury* was "steering very badly," and conditions were favorable for *Constitution*, whose course was southwest. With the wind generally northwest at speeds between seven and sixteen knots, she was able to make the most of her potential.

In the light of modern travel this potential does not seem very fast. Depending on the velocity and direction of the wind, the best a vessel like *Constitution* could do would approach something like twelve knots. In March of 1862, the rebuilt *Constellation* had caught the tail end of a spring storm and traveled from Portsmouth, New Hampshire, to the Azores in ten days, making good eleven knots for most of the way, but this was a record passage, unusual then and now. And it should be remembered that *Constellation* employed her full inventory of sails, had a full crew and was not burdened with a cargo.

The first indication that afternoon that things might not go precisely according to the plan ordained by higher authority was when the four to eight watch was set to bending on additional sails, putting on the main spencer and fore and main topmast staysails. The spencer was flown from a boom on the after side of the mainmast; the others were fastened to stays running to the masts named. All ran fore and aft, in contradiction to the sails set on the square yards. These new sails, which enabled her to point higher into the wind, undoubtedly helped her since the wind had begun to head her slightly. Shortly after that the log records, "The steamer unable to keep ahead of the ship" and, in addition, was "steering badly." Finally, at 6:30 that evening, the tow line was let go and *Constitution* was on her own. Commander Johnson may possibly have regretted his decision almost immediately. The winds had been getting lighter as the afternoon progressed; at 6 p.m. his speed was one knot, at 7 it was zero.

The probabilities are, however, that he had no such regrets. At 7 it began to rain and the wind, which had begun to swing to the southwest, went back to the northwest and increased somewhat in velocity. By 8 p.m. *Constitution's* speed went up to four knots and by 10 to six knots. What had happened was a phenomenon familiar to any sailor familiar with the area. A weak weather front had passed through, clearing the air, followed by a moderate to strong northwest wind, ideal for *Constitution's* course. Favored by such conditions, in the vernacular, the old lady picked up her skirts and ran.

By one in the morning of the 11th, *Constitution's* speed had reached seven knots and it varied between seven and eight knots for the next ten hours. During this period the wind alternated between force 4 and force 5, a range of thirteen to twenty-four miles per hour, holding at force 4 for six hours before rising to force 5 for the next four. With just a couple of exceptions *Constitution* ran at either seven or eight knots, but never less than seven, for the entire twenty-four hours at an average speed of seven and a half knots. Her noon position that day was calculated to be Latitude 39°43'N, Longitude 72°54'W. This position placed her some sixty miles off Barnegat Inlet, New Jersey, the scene of one of her more noteworthy exploits fifty-three years earlier.

During the War of 1812, Captain Isaac Hull had taken *Constitution* up the eastern seaboard from Annapolis to Boston. Off the coast of New Jersey he encountered what he believed to be an American squadron outward bound from New York to raid British commerce. Steering for them in light airs, he discovered at the last minute that the vessels were not the squadron which he had expected, but a British fleet sailing to intercept them. Outsailing his pursuers in light airs which lasted three days, *Constitution* had finally pulled away from them by a combination of sailing skill and trickery displayed by Isaac Hull. Observing a squall coming toward them, Hull boldly commenced furling his sails as rapidly as he could, imitated in this by the pursuing British, who could not see that the coming squall was merely a minor disturbance. As soon as *Constitution* was hidden from his pursuers by the rain, Hull clapped on all the sail he could muster and headed away as fast as he could. By the time the British realized what had happened Hull was beyond reach, heading for Boston and his forthcoming rendezvous with *Guerriere*, one of the vessels which had chased him. It had been this feat and the destruction of *Guerriere* which had first endeared *Constitution* to the American people.

This day's sail must have been a delight to those on board, particularly the children among the passengers, to whom this was a novelty. Only those who have experienced the joys of perfect sailing can truly comprehend what sheer delight it can be to have a good, sound vessel, warm pleasant weather, a fair wind and a kindly sea. The novice may conceive that a perfect sail consists of drifting dreamily down wind. Far from it; downwind sailing is dullness personified. But when the wind is abeam or a little abaft and is of sufficient force to move the vessel at her optimum speed, when the weather is warm and pleasant and the sea is just disturbed enough to make it challenging, then the ship comes to life and the world suddenly takes on new meaning.

It must not be thought that the ship remains steady as a rock or level as a table. No, the vessel has a soul of her own; she heels to the angle which best permits her to glide easily through the water, yielding to it while overcoming its resistance, mastering it in the end. All of this is done peacefully, yet not quietly. The wind is never silent; it varies in volume and intensity. Yet it always makes itself heard, pleasantly on days like these; fiercely on other days, and terrifying in its ultimate phase. And since that day was warm and clear, with scattered clouds painting moving shadows of light and darkness on the blue waters of the sea, it must have seemed like a dream to those fortunate passengers who experienced it. And *Constitution* was big and steady enough so that the landlubbers, particularly the children, could avoid seasickness.

Under such ideal conditions did *Constitution* move, all day long, into the night and all the following morning. Her last recorded position, at noon of the 12th, was Latitude 37°15'N, Longitude 75°W, a run of 150 miles. Now, 150 miles a day is no world shaking record. Old *Constitution*, herself, had done better, and there were times when the great clipper ships of the forties and fifties had done twice that. But what made this trip so notable was that she had run the steamer out of sight; she did it under far less sail than she might have carried, and she did it with less than a full crew.

The noonday run was her last at that speed. By one in the afternoon it had dropped, first to five and then to four knots, but that was an anticlimax. At 2:20 she sighted Cape Charles light; at 3:30 she made out Cape Henry Light, and at eleven that night she dropped anchor in Hampton Roads, three and a half days out of Newport—no record by any means, but a most satisfactory and fulfilling voyage.

She would live to make other voyages including a celebrated one to France in 1878, carrying exhibits to the Paris Exposition, but this one just may have been her most gratifying. She had run a steamship out of sight and had done it with only a portion of her strength and with a reduced crew.

Ten hours later *Mercury* came huffing and puffing into harbor. The day after that, she took back the tow line from *Constitution* and towed her up to the Naval Academy and into history.

*   *   *

The idea for this story came from *A Most Fortunate Ship* (Globe Pequot Press, 1980), a delightful history of the USS *Constitution*, written by one of her recent commanding officers, Commander

USS Constitution *(center) rests safely at her berth at Annapolis, after having spent the Civil War at Newport, Rhode Island.*

Tyrone G. Martin USN (Ret.). Details of *Constitution*'s sail plan may be found in *Dictionary of American Fighting Ships*, Vol. II, page 176. Facts respecting both the preparation for the trip and the voyage itself, including the wind and weather, are from the ship's deck log in the National Archives.

CHAPTER XVIII

Into the New Navy

In 1865 Gideon Welles was given a new task. Having labored long and hard in 1861 and 1862 to create an adequate navy for the Union, and equally long and hard the following two years to make his navy into an efficient and deadly weapon, he was now, in the post war period, required to dismantle his creation and replace it with a new and leaner peacetime navy. A victorious peace made his task more palatable but not easier. The number of men had to be reduced while retaining in the regular navy the best officers obtainable from what had become a proficient, but now too large, officer corps.

*　　*　　*

A navy that comprised 1457 officers and 7600 men at the outset of the Civil War had grown to 7500 volunteer officers and 51,500 men.[1] It had progressed from sail to steam to armor, and had become, by the end of the war, arguably the best navy in the world. Now, just at its apex, it faced the dilemma of how to reduce in numbers without a similar reduction in quality, and how to do so with fairness.

At the outset of the war the officer corps was composed entirely of professionals. This group had been diminished during the war by adherence to the Confederacy, by death and disability (whether service connected or not) or by promotion, all leaving vacancies in the lower ranks. These gaps, together with the vacancies created simply by the expansion of the service, were filled by volunteers drawn primarily from the merchant marine. Since many of them wished to remain in the post war navy, the best of these volunteers had to be integrated into the ranks of the regular officers.

It is fortunate that Welles, who had presided over the expansion of the navy during the war, presided over its reduction and subsequent reconstruction, for he had an overview of the whole process. He, himself, laid out the problem in his Annual Report for the year 1866:

> Where all had done so well, it was a delicate and embarrassing duty to discriminate and select for promotion. No body of men ever acquitted themselves with more honor than the gallant officers of the navy during the late war[2]

To assist Welles in this unpleasant task, Congress passed a statute on 25 July 1866 creating a board to examine volunteer officers desiring to apply for permanent commissions. To head the board Welles chose Commodore S. Phillips Lee. Lee was not a favorite of Welles, who had been dissatisfied with his performance when in command of the North Atlantic Blockading Squadron. The secretary had further objected to Lee's using the political influence of his father-in-law, Montgomery Blair, head of the politically powerful Blair family, to further his own ambitious ends and he eventually replaced him with Rear Admiral David D. Porter. Welles expressed his reservations about Lee in his diary:

> Had a call from my old friend the elder Blair. It was not unexpected. Detaching Lee from the North Atlantic Squadron I supposed would cause dissatisfaction to Lee, who would, through his wife, stimulate her father to make an effort in his behalf. The old man got word to-day that Lee was detached and hastened to me. He thought himself hard used in the blows that fell upon his children...I told him...that Lee was not degraded in being assigned to another command. I knew him to be cautious and vigilant, but not, perhaps the man for an immediate demonstration, an assault requiring prompt action. He had labored well, and in a pecuniary

point of view had been better paid than any man in the Navy...* Acting Admiral Lee has acquitted himself very well—as discharged his duties intelligently and firmly. But he can never be a great commander. While he has administered the affairs of his squadron safely, he has failed to devise and execute any important act....His caution runs into timidity...[3]

Lee was particularly galled by Welles' refusal to promote him to rear admiral's rank, particularly since he had held that acting rank during the war and had then reverted to captain, later commodore. In 1866 Lee and the Blairs continued to press for this promotion, which Welles declined because of Lee's inadequate combat experience. As a compromise, Welles offered him command of the Mare Island, California, Navy Yard. Lee first turned it down, then changed his mind, to the exasperation of Welles.[4] His diary is so full of complaints about Lee that one wonders why the man was employed at all.[5]

To assist Lee, Welles appointed Captain Foxhall A. Parker and Commander John Lee Davis, later joined by Captain Daniel Ammen and Commanders Walter W. Queen and K. Randolph Breese. Facing this formidable panel of experienced veterans, all of whom had seen considerable action during the war, was certain to provide a daunting experience. The board chose Hartford, Ct., a point deemed to be a central location between Philadelphia, Pa., and Portsmouth N.H., but hardly a seaport, as the site for its activities. No explanation is given for choosing Philadelphia and Portsmouth. The probable reason may be that the entire South was still an occupied territory.

Many regular navy officers, of course, opposed the idea of the board.[6] To ensure impartiality and counter the mistrust the con-

---

* Lee, as commander of the North Atlantic Squadron, was entitled to a percentage of the value of all ships and cargoes captured by the vessels of his squadron and this had made him a very wealthy man by the standards of the time.

Although it was not to fight another major sea battle until 1898, the U.S. Navy fully understood the future of naval warfare, as these test firings against armor plate at the Washington Navy Yard in July 1866 clearly show.

cept had engendered, Welles, on 27 August 1866, set forth in minute detail how the board was to proceed. Thus the board was instructed to:

1. Cause each applicant to pass a physical examination.
2. If the applicant passed, he was to "retire to an adjoining room, furnished with writing material, to prepare, unaided by either book or

the writing of his preference," a resumè reciting his age, experience in the navy and merchant marine, and what languages, if any, he spoke.

The applicant was then to be given written examinations in the following subjects: arithmetic, geography, English composition, steam, French and Spanish.

Members of the board were then to examine him orally in seamanship, navigation, naval gunnery, naval tactics and naval routine. Welles, hoping the board could mitigate the popular dislike of the project, added: "The Board will endeavor to relieve candidates of all embarrassment, and to encourage them to calmly consider every question propounded before answering it." The board's mandate was "to select and report to the Secretary of the Navy the most meritorious in character, ability, professional competence and honorable service." Names were to be reported "in order of merit," which the board interpreted to mean according to the value of the final grade. Names of those found not qualified were to be reported in the same manner.

The board assigned to each subject a perfect grade, then agreed upon a minimum passing grade. The grades assigned are revealing (see Table I). It further determined that anyone who attained a perfect score, or 2753, would be deemed qualified for appointment to the rank of lieutenant commander. Since only God Himself could possibly have attained a perfect grade, in the end, no one qualified for the rank of lieutenant commander, which left God in command of the universe and the admirals in command of the navy, presumably to everyone's satisfaction.

The examination gives us some insight into what the board really expected of a naval officer. Of the fifteen subjects tested, eight carried a minimum passing grade of zero, implying that the board deemed these subjects not to be absolutely required of a naval officer. One of these was steam, even five years after *Monitor* and *Virginia* had demonstrated that the days of fighting sail were over forever. The board appears to have been given what today seems an excessive amount of discretion since so much of the examination was oral. Opportunities for favoritism were tremendous. The applicants, drawn from the ranks of practical seamen possessing little formal education had to answer questions such as these:

Arithmetic:

- Multiply eighty-seven million six hundred and nine by forty-five thousand three hundred and seventy (spelled out).
- If $\frac{3}{8}$ of an acre cost 624 dollars what will $\frac{7}{8}$ of an acre cost?

Geography:

- What countries of Europe border on the Atlantic? What on the Mediterranean? What on the Baltic Sea?
- Designate the countries which furnish coffee; those which furnish tea; and those which furnish opium; those which grow cotton, tobacco and sugar.
- Which are the great grain growing powers?

Seamanship:

- How would you mast a ship with a pair of shears in a stream?

Naval Gunnery:

- How would you arm and station an XI inch gun crew left hand side commencing at the muzzle?

From a list of thirty questions about steam, the applicant could choose any fifteen such as:

- What are the principal parts of a steam engine?
- When boilers foam, what should be done and what is understood by foam?
- How is steam combined in low pressure?

The characteristics of ability, honorable service and character, for which no minimum standards appear to have been set, carried a combined weight of 1514 out of 2753; seamanship carried an additional weight of 354. Thus it was perfectly possible to award commissions to persons with great practical experience but little formal education.

With all these apparently obvious defects, it is difficult to quarrel with the board's philosophy. The pool from which appointments were to be made was composed of individuals possessing practical experience as opposed to "book learning." And, after all, the applicants had demonstrated their ability by their active service in the war.

The board took almost two years to finally complete its job. Its slowness is understandable; procedures had to be established, notice given throughout the service, applications received, and the applicants brought to the testing site. At the same time the tests had to be distributed to applicants on foreign service, who were examined by mail.

At the conclusion of its task the board filed its report and accompanying documents with the Secretary of the Navy. These may be found today in the National Archives as Entry 166, Record Group 45. They consist of six very dusty bound volumes of assorted sizes and conditions. Included therein are all the questions and answers from, at least, the overseas officers taking the examination by mail.

In all, 466 applied and 238 were examined. The board recommended 68 for appointment to the following ranks: Lieutenant (7); Master (16) and Ensign (45). Acting Volunteer Lieutenant Nehemiah H. Dyer, the high scorer, was recommended for appointment as a lieutenant, hardly surprising in view of his service during the war. Entering the service in April 1862 as a mate, he had been promoted acting master in January 1864 and acting volunteer lieutenant in April 1865; he had been commended by his division commander for gallantry off Fort Morgan in Mobile Bay.*

---

* His subsequent service was as distinguished as his earlier. He commanded *Baltimore* at the battle of Manila Bay in 1898, was advanced in relative rank for his conduct in that engagement and retired as a rear admiral.

The board duly listed all the rest in order of grade and was discharged from its thankless and difficult task. Captain Daniel Ammen, a member of the board later indicated his satisfaction:

> To officer [the newly enlisted men] intelligent officers and seamen from the merchant service were sought, who, after passing examinations to establish their professional fitness, were given acting appointments in various grades. It is proper to add that as a whole they fairly fulfilled reasonable expectations, and after the war was over and passing other examinations, more than fifty of these volunteer officers, many of whom would do honor to any navy, entered the regular service.

There seems to have been little discrimination towards the sixty-eight new appointees. One officer, for example, who had enlisted as a seaman in November 1861 was appointed to the grade of master in 1867 after he stood fourteenth on the list. He was promoted to lieutenant in 1868 and to lieutenant commander in 1870, an advancement scarcely possible had there been real prejudice against the newly absorbed officers. All in all, Lee and his fellow officers seem to have performed their duties fairly and capably, to their great credit and the greater good of the service.

Comparison of Board Criteria with Scores of Highest Applicant, Acting Volunteer Lieutenant Nehemiah M. Dyer.			
SUBJECT	MINIMUM TO PASS	PERFECT SCORE	HIGHEST SCORE (DYER)
Applicant's record	0	25	23
Algebra	23	39	39
Arithmetic	0	80	79
Geometry	0	100	100
Geography	25	45	41.5
English composition	14	25	18
Steam	0	125	102
French	0	88	72
Spanish	0	48	15
Seamanship	212	354	284
Navigation	84	140	124
Gunnery	72	120	106
Naval tactics & routine	27	50	44
Total of the Above	457	1239	1049
Ability	0	714	590
Honorable service & character	0	800	627
Final Score	457	2753	2274

Sources

There are two major sources of information for this work. The first is *The Official Records of the Union and Confederate Navies in the War of the Rebellion* (ORN). The compilers of this work, whose collective efforts spanned several decades, performed a monumental task and did it well. While probably not every minute memorandum was included, more than enough material was compiled to present in detail a panorama of the naval war. In addition to official reports themselves, from time to time, extraneous material such as a clipping from a newspaper, a private letter or extracts from a diary, will be encountered. All such material appearing here is derived from that source.

The second source is the deck logs of the vessels involved. By the time of the Civil War, the routine of keeping an accurate record of happenings at sea had become systematized to the degree that the accuracy of these reports can be considered reliable. In contrast, *Constitution*'s 1812 log of her famous battle with HMS *Guerriere* is so sparse in its account of the battle as to convey almost none of the details, let alone the flavor.

Although possible biases of the writers must obviously be taken into account, the amount of detail required to be entered—hourly recordings of the course, speed, wind, and weather for example—made it difficult, if not impossible, to depart too far from the truth. Those deck logs are admissible in evidence to this day in any court in the United States as records kept in the ordinary course of business.

Most of these logs will be found in the National Archives, although some are absent. Those of *Monitor* and *Housatonic*, for instance, must have gone down with the ships; the absence of others is not explained. Those present are available for study, the closest we can get to those long gone participants.

Biographical data concerning officers has been taken from Callaghan, *List of Officers of the Navy of the United States and of the Marine Corps from 1775 to 1900*, originally published by L. R. Hamersly, N. Y. in 1901, reprinted by Olde Soldier Books, Inc. (There is a nostalgic link between that time and our own towards the end of the book when, listed as "Naval Cadets, 1900" appears the name of William F. Halsey of World War II fame.)

Ships' data may be found in at least three places. The first is in ORN II, Volume 1. A much more complete source is Silverstone, *Warships of the Civil War Navies*, Naval Institute Press, 1989. A third is in the very complete *Dictionary of American Fighting Ships*, published by the Navy Department. I have used all three but, primarily, Silverstone because his work is both complete and compact.

I have used the writings of two individuals who played an important part in the Civil War. The diary of Secretary of the Navy Gideon Welles, published in 1911 by Houghton Mifflin Company, has been a gold mine of material ever since it came to light. If he had an appropriate comment, I used it. The other, that of Admiral David D. Porter, is probably the one participant I would most like to have interviewed personally. His highly selective memory make both his *Incidents and Anecdotes of the Civil War*, published in 1885, and *The Naval History of the Civil War*, published in 1886 by the Sherman Publishing Company, suspect, and his highly entertaining works should be taken with a grain of salt. He is masterful in the wording of his reports and orders.

For information on CSS *Florida*, in addition to the material in ORN, I went to Cochran, *Blockade Runners of the Confederacy*, Bobbs-Merrill, 1958. As to stormy Charles Wilkes, I relied on ORN and an article in the United States Naval Institute *Proceed-*

ings, Vol. 57, No. 7, July, 1931, entitled *Charles Wilkes, Turbulent Scholar of the Old Navy.*

Wilkes' court martial record has been printed as Ex. Doc. No. 103, 38th Congress, 1st Session. Unless you are intrigued by the stilted language of the English common law, I would advise avoiding it. It is a classic example of the turgidity which modern lawyers have long since thrown away.

*   *   *

Books

Callaghan, *List of Officers of the Navy of the United States and of the Marine Corps from 1795 to 1900,* L. R. Hamersly, 1901, Olde Soldier Reprint.

Cochran, *Blockade Runners of the Confederacy,* Bobbs-Merrill, 1958.

Cornish and Laas, *Lincoln's Lee,* University of Kansas Press, 1986.

Diary of Gideon Welles, Houghton Mifflin Co., 1911.

The Commodores, Guttredge and Smith, Harper & Row, 1969.

Navy Department, *Dictionary of American Fighting Ships,* Government Printing Office.

Official Records of the Union and Confederate Navies in the War of the Rebellion, 30 volumes plus index, Government Printing Office, 1894-1921.

Porter, *Incidents and Anecdotes of the Civil War,* D. Appleton and Company, 1885.

Porter, *The Naval History of the Civil War,* Sherman Publishing Co., 1886.

Pratt, *The Navy, A History,* Garden City Publishing Co., 1941.

Regulations for the Government of the Navy, April 18, 1865, Government Printing Office, No. 151.

Report of the Lee Board, National Archives, Entry 166, Record Group 45.

Silverstone, *Warships of the Civil War Navies,* Naval Institute Press, 1989.

Articles or Other Documents

Annual Report of the Secretary of the Navy, 1863, House Executive Documents, 38th Congress, Doc. 1, IV, pp. xxiii-xxiv.

Annual Report of the Secretary of the Navy, Dec. 6, 1866.

Bennett, *Principles of Internal Medicine*. McGraw-Hill, 1958, p. 1184.

Commodore Charles Wilkes's Court Martial, House Executive Documents, 38th Congress, 1st Session, Doc. 102, XV, 133.

Ericcson, "The Building of the *Monitor*, I *Battles and Leaders*, 730.

Farenholt, Adm. A., *William Conway, Naval Hero*, submission to the Secretary of the Navy, in file on USS *Conway*, Old Ships files, Naval Historical Center, Washington Navy Yard.

Greene, "The *Monitor* At Sea and in Battle," Naval Institute *Proceedings*, November, 1923, p. 1839.

Lawson, "It happened in Bahia," Naval Institute *Proceedings*, June, 1932, pp. 834-836.

Martin, "When the *Monitor* Went Down," Naval Institute *Proceedings*, July, 1941, p. 927.

McMaster, "A Little Unwritten History of the Original USS *Monitor*, Naval Institute *Proceedings*, Issue No. 100, p. 725 (1901).

Soley, "The Confederate Cruisers," IV *Battles and Leaders*, Century, 1887, Castle Reprint, 1983, p.595.

Soley, "The Union and Confederate Navies," I *Battles and Leaders*, 623.

Notes

Chapter I

1. O.R.N. I, 4, 41.
2. Taken from an undated paper written by Rear Admiral A. Farenholt, Medical Corps USN, submitted in support of his suggestion that a World War II destroyer be named after Conway. This paper is in the Old Ships file at the Office of Naval History in the Washington Navy Yard.
3. O.R.N. I, 4, 55.

Chapter II

1. The committee divided its report into several sections, each dealing with a specific portion of the coast. The section dealing with the Head of the Passes appears in ORN I, 16, 618.
2. ORN I, 16, 683.
3. *Ibid.*, 699.
4. *Ibid.*, 711.
5. *Ibid.*, 703 *et seq.*

Chapter III

1. All quotations are from the reports of Weidman and Ringgold in O.R.N. I, 12, 232 *et seq.* or from the rather scant deck log of *Sabine* in the National Archives

Chapter IV

1. Platt, *The Navy, a History*, Garden City Publishing Co., Inc., 1941, p. 226.
2. All quotations are either taken from the ship's deck log now in the National Archives or from the report of the incident in *The Official Records*

of the Union and Confederate Navies in the War of the Rebellion (ORN) Series I, Vol. 1, pp. 335 et. seq. under the heading "The Search for the US Ship *Vermont*, March 1 to April 12 1862." Spelling appears as in the original.

3. Luce, *Seamanship*, Van Nostrand & Company 1866, p. 546.

Chapter V

1. *The Official Records of the Union and Confederate Navies in the War of the Rebellion (ORN), Series I*, Vol. 6, p. 64.
2. *Ibid.*, 72.
3. *Ibid.*, 78.
4. *Ibid.*, 713.
5. *Ibid.*, 121.
6. Porter, *Naval History of the Civil War*, Sherman Publishing Company, 1886, p. 45.
7. ORN I, 6, 141.
8. Holzman, *Stormy Ben Butler*, Collier Books, 1954, p. 63.
9. ORN I, 6, 122.
10. *Ibid.*, 133.

Chapter VI

1. *The Official Records of the Union and Confederate Navies in the War of the Rebellion (ORN), Series I*, Vol. 7, p. 99.
2. *Ibid.*
3. *Ibid.*, 99, 100.
4. *Ibid.*, 126.
5. *Ibid.*, 129.
6. *(ORN), Series I*, Vol. 7, p. 745, *ibid*, p. 745.
7. *Ibid*, p. 746.
8. *Ibid.*, 331.
9. *The Official Records of the Union and Confederate Armies in the War of the Rebellion* (ORA), Series I, Part 1, p. 634 *et seq.*
10. *Battles and Leaders of the Civil War*, 1983 reprint, Vol. II page 152.
11. *Ibid.*, 7, 337.
12. *Ibid.*, 7, 798.
13. ORA I, 11, Part 1, 634.

14. ORN I, 6, 168.
15. *Ibid.*, 310.

Chapter VII

1. The others were *Merrimack* (later CSS *Virginia*), *Minnesota*, *Roanoke* and *Colorado*. All served in the Civil War and only *Merrimack* failed to survive it. *Roanoke* became unique when she was converted to the only three turreted vessel in the navy.
2. Pratt, *The Navy, a History*, Garden City Publishing Co., 1941, p. 255
3. This and all other quotations are taken from the deck log of *Wabash* now in the National Archives in Washington.
4. ORN I, 10, 564.
5. Deck log of *Saugus*, National Archives.

Chapter VIII

1. *Maria's* log, in the National Archives, corroborates this comment. Noon positions are rarely given; on 11 December, for example, longitude is omitted.
2. ORN I, 17, 3.
3. *Ibid.*, 18, 480.

Chapter IX

1. Extracted from an article by Ivan L. Bennett, Jr., in *Principles of Internal Medicine*, McGraw-Hill, 1958, p. 1184.
2. Report of *Roebuck's* commanding officer to the Secretary of the Navy, Sept. 28, 1864, ORN I,17, 761.
3. See reports, Greene to Welles and Nickerson to Greene, ORN I, 17, 744 followed by report, Eldredge to Welles, *ibid*, 748.
4. From *Chambers'* deck log in the National Archives.
5. *Ibid.*
6. ORN 1, 19, 265, 290.

Chapter X

1. The redress would come years later when damage caused by her was included in the *Alabama* Claims arbitration which concluded favorably to the United States.

2. *Diary of Gideon Welles*, Houghton Mifflin Co., 1911, Vol. 1, p. 141.

3. *Ibid.*

4. ORN I, 1, 440 *et seq.*

5. Sicard had previously been in command in August, 1862 while waiting for Preble to report. He had more than one frustration during his career. He was in command of the North Atlantic Squadron at the outbreak of the Spanish-American War but illness forced him to turn it over to Rear Admiral William T. Sampson who thus became the commander in the battle of Santiago de Cuba.

6. Less than a year had elapsed since the inception of the *Trent* affair had embarrassed the Federal government.

7. ORN I, 2, 622.

8. Following his retirement he published three books, a biography of Rear Admiral Henry K. Thatcher, a chronology of the opening of Japan and a history of the American flag. Curiously enough his old command *Oneida* met the same fate as her nemesis *Florida*. She was rammed and sunk in Yokohama Bay, Japan in 1870.

9. Perhaps there was a tinge of smugness in Maffitt's voice when, asked whether the log of *Florida* was in the Navy or the State Department, he replied, "It is not in either; it was dropped in fifteen fathoms off Charleston." Towards the end of the war Maffitt returned to the command of blockade runners and when on one occasion it appeared likely that he would be captured his quartermaster jettisoned a weighted bag containing Maffitt's journal and the log of *Florida*.

10. Porter, *The Naval History of the Civil War*, Sherman Publishing Co. 1886.

11. Cochran, *Blockade Runners of the Confederacy*, Bobbs-Merrill, 1958, p. 263.

12. Emmons, while never achieving the fame of some of his contemporaries, had a distinguished naval career. He had been a midshipman in the steam frigate *Fulton* when she blew up in 1828 and later accompanied then Lieutenant Charles Wilkes in his Antarctic expedition. Later in this war he became Fleet Captain (Chief of Staff) under Rear Admiral John A. Dahlgren off Charleston in 1864. While in command of *R. R. Cuyler* he captured Cedar Keys and Pass Christian plus "some twenty prizes." He had twenty three years' sea duty and eleven years shore duty, a record any man could be proud of.

13. ORN I, 19, 528 &c.

14. *Ibid.*, I, 2, 28.

15. *Ibid* I, 19, 528&c.

16. Porter, *The Naval History of the Civil War*, Sherman Publishing Co., 1886, p. 627.

17. Porter, *op. cit*, 623. In addition, Semmes' statements and writings concerning the *Alabama*'s cruise and defeat indicate that he simply was a sore loser.

18. *Ibid.*, 625

19. Entry of Aug. 10, 1862, *Diary of Gideon Welles*, Houghton Mifflin Company 1911, Vol. 1 p. 73.

20. Entry of Sept. 4, 1862, id., p. 109.

21. O.R.N., I, 1. 470.

22. Fox's testimony, *Commodore Charles Wilkes's Court Martial*, House Executive Documents, 38th Cong. 1st Sess., Doc. 102, XV, 133.

23. O.R.N. I, 2, 60.

24. O.R.N I, 1, 496.

25. O.R.N I, 2, 116.

26. O.R.N I, 2, 135.

27. Wilkes to Welles, Jan,. 29, 1863, O.R.N I, 2, 54.

28. Wilkes to Welles, Dec. 4, 1862, O.R.N. I,1571.

29. Wilkes to Welles, Jan. 23, 1863, O.R.N. I,1,54.

30. Welles to Wilkes, O.R.N. I,2,113.

31. Welles to Wilkes, O.R.N. I,2, 182.

32. Wilkes to Welles, O.R.N. I,2,353.

33. Farragut to Welles, June 23, 1863, O.R.N I,2,535.

34. Baldwin to Welles, O.R.N. I,2,138.

35. Pratt, *The Navy, a History*, Garden City Publishing Co., 1941, p. 299.

36. *Report of the Secretary of the Navy, 1863*, House Executive Documents, 38th Cong. 1st Sess., Doc. 1, IV, pp. xxiii-xxiv.

37. Wilkes to Welles, O.R.N. I,25 67.

38. Wilkes to Welles, Dec. 15, 1863, O.R.N. I,2,569

39. *Commodore Charles Wilkes's Court Martial*, House Executive Documents, 38th Congress., 1st Sess., Doc 102, XV, 1-180.

40. *Regulations for the Government of the Navy*, April 18, 1865, Government Printing Office, Regulation No. 151, p. 26.

41. Born Pa. Midshipman 1-2-1834; Passed mid. 7-16-40; Master 8-15-46;

Lt. 11-6-46; Cdr. 9-16-52; Capt. 7-25-66; Commo. 1-19-71; RADM 8-19-74. Died 8-9-75.

42. *It Happened in Bahia* by Lt. Raymond S. Lawson, USNR, U.S. Naval Institute Proceedings, June, 1932 (Whole No. 352), pp. 834-836 is a narrative of the event as related to the author by his father, a member of *Wachusett's* crew. Her deck log does not mention engine repairs but they could well have taken place, since she was in the act of replacing her bowsprit, and there was ample time for engine repairs.

43. ORN I, 3, 631 *et seq.*

44. *Kearsarge* had defeated and sunk *Alabama* off Cherbourg, France, 19 June 1864.

45. From the deck log of *Wachusett* in the National Archives.

46. ORN I, 3, 637

47. *Diary of Gideon Welles*, (Houghton Mifflin Co., 1911) Vol. II. p. 185, entry of November 26, 1864.

48. Porter, *The Naval History of the Civil War*, Sherman Publishing Co. 1886, p. 816.

49. ORN I, 3, 274.

50. *Ibid.*

51. Porter. *op. cit.*, 816.

52. ORN I, 3, 268.

Chapter XI

1. A record of the weather is contained in an abstract from the deck log of *Housatonic* which was forwarded by Admiral Du Pont to the Navy Department as a part of the record of the court of inquiry, ORN I, 13, 58. The original deck log of that vessel probably went down with her when she was torpedoed off Charleston 17 February 1864,

2. From Stellwagen's graphic report in ORN I, 13, 579.

3. *Ibid.*, 617, 618.

4. *Ibid.*, 580.

5. *Ibid.*, 584.

6. *Ibid.*, 586.

7. *Ibid.*, 619. Tucker's last sentence appears to contradict his earlier statements.

8. *Ibid.*, 617. However, Beauregard's telegrams to Richmond earlier that day demonstrate his own doubts as to the truthfulness of that proclamation.

9. *Ibid.*, 612.

10. *Diary of Gideon Welles*, Houghton Mifflin Company, 1913, vol. I, p. 232, entry of 4 February 1863.

Chapter XII

1. *The Official Records of the Union and Confederate Navies in the War of the Rebellion (ORN), Series I*, Vol. 2, pp. 648, 649.

2. *Ibid.*, 274, 275, 276.

3. *Ibid.*, 300-314 *passim.*

4. *Ibid.*, 300 *et seq.*

5. ORN I, 7, 420.

6. *Diary of Gideon Welles*, Houghton Mifflin Company, New York 1911, Vol. I, p. 347.

7. ORN I, 2, 333. See, for example, the order of Commodore Montgomery to the acting master of the schooner *J. S. Baker* dated 29 June 1863 appearing on page 335.

8. Silverstone, *Warships of the Civil War*, Naval Institute Press, 1989, pp. 187 *et seq.*

Chapter XIII

1. Parker's order or "commission" appears in full in ORN I, 2, 541.

2. Deck log of *Dacotah* now in the National Archives.

3. Clary's report, ORN I, 2, 528.

4. Nickel's report, ORN I, 2, 526.

5. *Diary of Gideon Welles*, Houghton Mifflin Company, 1911, p. 490, entry of 19 December 1863.

6. ORN I, 2, 530.

Chapter XIV

1. ORN I, 11, 214.

2. *Ibid.*, 216.

3. Midshipman, 1829. Passed Midshipman, 1835; Lieutenant, 1841; Commander, 1861; Rear Admiral, 1863 (he never served in the rank of Captain); Vice Admiral, 1866; Admiral, 1870. Died 13 February 1891. Founder, United States Naval Institute.

4. *Incidents and Anecdotes of the Civil War*, Appleton and Company, 1885.

5. *Ibid.*, 267, 268.
6. The entire order is set out in ORN I, 11, 222.
7. *Ibid.*, 237.
8. *Naval History of the Civil War*, 692, 696.

Chapter XV

1. Thomas T, Craven. Midshipman, 1 May, 1822; Passed Mid. 24 May, 1828; Lieut. 27 May, 1830; Commander, 16 Dec. 1852; Captain, 7 June, 1861; Commodore, 16 July, 1862; RADM, 10 Oct, 1866; Retired List, 30 Dec. 1869; died 23 Aug. 1887. Not to be confused with the Commander Tunis A.M. Craven ("After you, pilot"), who went down heroically in *Tecumseh* at Mobile Bay in 1864.
2. ORN I, 1, 18, 604.
3. The entire affair appears in O.R.N. I, 3, 461 *et seq.*, commencing with Craven's report.
4. ORN I, 3, 464.
5. *Ibid.*, 461.
6. *Diary of Gideon Welles*, Houghton Mifflin Company, 1911, Vol. 2, pp. 261, 267.
7. Welles, *op. cit.*, 392.
8. *Ibid.*, 396.
9. Porter, *The Naval History of the Civil War*, Sherman Publishing Company, 1885.

Chapter XVI

1. Figures taken from an article by Soley, *The Union and Confederate Navies*, I *Battles and Leaders* 623.
2. *Annual Report of the Secretary of the Navy*, 3 December, 1866.
3. *Diary of Gideon Welles*, Houghton Mifflin Company, 1911, Vol II, p. 161, entry of 27 September 1864
4. *Ibid.*, p. 513, entry of 28 May 1866.
5. The facts are recounted in detail in Cornish and Laas, *Lincoln's Lee*, University of Kansas Press, 1986, pp. 159 *et set.*
6. Cornish and Laas affirm that it was, *op. cit.*, p. 159 and there is no reason to disagree. The officers surviving from the Old Navy most likely had been welded into a clique which would resent the volunteer officers.

INDEX